Understanding Chinese Characters
by their Ancestral Forms

Fourth Edition

By
Ping-gam Go

SIMPLEX PUBLICATIONS
Larkspur, CA

This book is dedicated to my two lovely grandchildren
Monika Tian Ming and Gavin Mai Lang

Other books by Ping-gam Go:
*What Character Is That? An Easy-Access Dictionary of 5,000 Chinese
    Characters*
Understanding Kanji Characters by their Ancestral Forms
Read Chinese Today

Understanding Chinese Characters by their Ancestral Forms
Fourth Edition
Copyright © 1977, 1978, 1987, 1988, 1989, 1992, 1995 by Gam P. Go
Copyright © 2004 by Gam Ping Go Declaration of Trust dated
    October 11, 2000

Fourth edition 2004
08 07 06 05 04   11 10 9 8 7 6

ISBN 0-9623113-7-5
Library of Congress Control Number: 2004092982

Simplex Publications
575 Larkspur Plaza, Suite 4
Larkspur, CA 94939
http://www.simplexpublications.com

Go, Ping-gam (1922-2000)
Subjects: Chinese language—Etymology
          Chinese characters
          Chinese language—Writing

Contents

Notes on the Fourth Edition

In 1966, my father, Ping-gam Go, brought his wife and three daughters from Amsterdam, The Netherlands to San Francisco's Bay Area. In spite of the fact that he spoke five languages and despite his Chinese heritage, he did not speak Chinese. He was a world traveler who lived in three continents, yet for the first time in his life, my father was unable to engage in conversation with the local people of San Francisco's Chinatown. My father's quest to learn Chinese was the genesis of Simplex Publications.

Trying to learn Chinese at the age of 44 proved to be extremely difficult for my father. He found the character strokes counterintuitive and nearly impossible to memorize. As he studied, he learned that the language was borne out of a more ancient form that was much more pictorial. Using the ancient strokes, he began to unravel the complexity of the Chinese characters. He was so proud when he mastered the first twenty characters that he made a chart depicting the ancient form next to the modern brush form, framed it, and hung it up on our living room wall. Not long after, he replaced this chart with one containing about 50 characters. This chart soon became the most frequent conversation piece in our house and many of our guests encouraged my father to write a book.

By 1976, he had written his first book, twelve pages of 100 simple Chinese characters consisting of 1 to 5 strokes. The next year, he founded Simplex Publications. During the next seven years, he self-published three very simple, but charming, staple-bound books which he gave away to friends and business clients: *How to Understand Chinese Characters by Means of their Ancient Symbols, Part 1: 1-5 Strokes, Part 2: 5-10 Strokes,* and *Part 3: over 10 Strokes.* In 1984, these books grew into his first commercial book, *How to Understand Chinese Characters by Means of their Ancestral Forms,* which is now presented its fourth edition: *Understanding Chinese Characters by Their Ancestral Forms.* In 1991, he published a tourist version of the book, named *Read Chinese Today,* which was both more compact and affordable.

By this time my father was beginning to make very good progress in his quest to learn Chinese. He was frustrated, however, with the way most Chinese dictionaries are organized because you had to know how many strokes a Chinese character has before you can look it up. As a result, he created a dictionary that was sorted by the name of the radical, or the root pictogram, of the character. In 1995, he published *What Character Is That? An Easy-Access Dictionary of 5,000 Chinese Characters*, now in its second edition. The dictionary was an immediate success, drawing many positive reviews.

Throughout the years, many members of the Japanese community urged my father to write similar books for Kanji characters. In 2000, Gam Go wrote *Understanding Kanji Characters by their Ancestral Forms, Learning Kanji through Pictures*. Suddenly, at the age of 78, he passed away, only weeks after submitting the book to the printer.

As my sisters and I worked to close up our father's home, the book printer notified us that the Kanji book was printed and ready to be picked up for distribution. At the same time, the fax machine spewed multiple orders from wholesale distributors. Not wanting to disappoint our father and his legacy, we worked hard to fill the orders in time for the Christmas rush. My sisters and I were in the publishing business!

Now I love showing my two young children the first simple give-away books their "Opa" created. This beginning demonstrates that, to be successful, you can start very small and very simply, as long as you follow your passion. My sisters and I plan to carry on this legacy of simplicity and passion through Simplex Publications.

Diana Go
(Go Tjing-Hian)
March 2004

Acknowledgments

I would like to acknowledge my three daughters, Sian, Lan, and Hian for their keen interest in the project and for their valuable contributions in submitting material for the manuscript and in making suggestions, corrections and improvements. In addition to this, Lan took part in the editing of the second edition; she also spent many hours of tediously cutting and accurately replacing the Chinese characters in the Subject Index and in the Table of Contents.

Janet Gardiner did the difficult proofreading of the Chinatown Walk chapter. Emily Wilcox was very helpful in putting critical portions of the text in correct and clear language.

George Yasukochi wrote a detailed analysis of the book with valuable suggestions for changes.

The brush-written characters (not the ancestral forms, which were done by myself) was the work of You-shan Tang, calligrapher.

Special thanks to Kathryn Dare for allowing me to use her drawing: "The Chinese Fortune Calendar" (page P32).

Bill Regan, Sr., Bill Regan, Jr., and Bert Ripple, through their interests and enthusiasms for the book in its early years, were instrumental in its gradual development.

The Chinatown Branch of the San Francisco Public Library was very helpful in providing me with the material to arrive at the Cantonese pronunciations of the characters in this Third Edition.

Last but not least, Jean and Sara Gabriel of European Book Company, Inc. gave valuable suggestions as to the format and marketing of the book when it first came out as "How to Understand Chinese Characters" in 1987.

To all of them, I would like to express my sincere gratitude and thanks.

Notes on the Third Edition

Appearing finally in color, the photos I took many years ago will induce more people to read this book, since put in their beautiful colored settings the characters are more appealing.

Other than that, the first part of the book remains virtually unchanged, most changes occurring in the Dictionary section. A new feature has been added, namely **Flash Cards** to be cut out (or highlighted) and used for review purposes.

To give the book a uniform appearance, the Dictionary has been reduced in size. However, for readability the size of the letters in the text has been kept the same. The characters themselves appear in large size on the Flash Cards at the end of the book. A thorough review of the text results in many changes meant to give better explanations to the meanings of the characters. Most changes are only minor in nature. The major changes are shown by character numbers followed by the meanings of the characters (see Footnotes below)[1].

A major change came as a result of an elaborate and enthusiastic letter from Maureen Porter, who rightfully so, pointed out that the character (No. 32) could also mean "Woman". The meaning of this character has now been changed from "Man" to "Man(kind), Woman, Person", resulting in the substitutions of "Man" to "Woman" or "Person(s)" in numerous other characters.

References to pages in the Walk through Chinatown chapter (marked as W13, etc.) have been introduced in the Dictionary, since a lot of additional information can be gathered from those places.[2]

Pronunciations of the characters, previously occurring as footnotes, now are made part of the main text. Following requests from various quarters, the Cantonese pronunciations are also included.

And lastly, the characters and letters in the Subject Index have been printed larger to make for easier reading.

Notes on the Second Edition

To make it easy to find sections in the *Walk through Chinatown* text frequently referred to in the book; the key characters are placed in boxes alongside the paragraphs in which they occur. Also you will find new characters discussed in the first part of the Photo Section.

All characters in the Character Finder are accompanied by their meanings. In many cases, you only want to know their meanings and this arrangement makes it in such cases unnecessary for you to consult the Dictionary. (Through the character numbers you can still find their additional meanings and their etymology in the Dictionary.)

---

[1] Corrections were made in the following characters: Nos. 11, 12, 83, 92 (Sea), 94, 98, 99, 100, 102, 151, 153 (Trade), 180, 213 (Wide), 214 (Peaceful), 223 (New), 232, 240, 242, 260 (Good), 262, 263 (Righteousness), 276, 278 (Not), 280, 288.

[2] "Man" or "Men" were changed to "Woman" or "Person(s)" in the following characters: Nos. 32 (Man), 41 (Crowd), 43 (Traveler), 46 (Empress), 118 (Pill), 139 (To manage), 145 (To lend), 148 (Beginning), 152 (Agriculture), 155 (Value), 161 (House), 184 (Long(time)), 190 (Night), 193 (Summer), 200 (North), 207 (Center), 208 (Big), 209 (Small), 211 (Top), 214 (To stand), 245 (To wander), 247 (Boundary, 262 (Love), 276 (To believe), 279 (To change).

To locate a character in the Character Finder, you have to know the number of strokes it contains. In "How to Use the Character Finder", you will find complete information on writing a Chinese character and on finding the number of strokes it contains.

An important addition has been made inasmuch as references to the photographs have been introduced in the Dictionary Section. The quality of the photographs has been highly improved by printing them through metal plates; and new photos have been introduced.

Following consultation with *A Chinese-English Dictionary,* published by the Beijing Foreign Language Institute, additional meanings have been introduced in the Dictionary Section and in the Subject Index.

And finally, in the Table of Contents and in the Subject Index all Chinese characters have been replaced by bigger and better ones.

Foreword

A number of books have been written dealing with the origin of Chinese characters. They explain the meaning of the modern brush writings on the basis of their ancestral forms. All are ultimately based in the classical lexicon *Shuo Wên Chieh Tzu* (freely translated: "On the interpretation of characters") written around the year 200 A.D. by a famous scholar named Hsü-hsên. To this day it has formed the basis of all research in etymology.

You will discover that it takes little effort and imagination to understand the most commonly seen characters, once you know their ancestral forms and their explanations.

This book is a follow-up course to my other book, *Read Chinese Today,* which discusses 68 common characters. In this book you will find the ancestral forms and explanation of 288 characters. With a knowledge of these characters, you will be able to understand most of the beautiful Chinese characters in San Francisco's Chinatown and in other American cities.

Introduction

Chinese characters – let's understand them !

Contrary to general belief, the Chinese writing system is not a complex system to be understood only by the Chinese . Far from that – it is an amazingly simple system which reveals the ingenuity of the ancient Chinese scholars. The complexity came about only after the writing brush transformed the original stylus pictures into puzzling entities.

The origin of Chinese characters goes far back to the early history of China some 5,000 years ago, around 3000 B.C., as can be established from inscriptions on oracle bones made of tortoise shells. During a later period, inscriptions were made on sacrificial vessels as a means to establish contact with the spirits of deceased loved ones. It was probably due to the need to communicate with invisible deities and spirits that a stylus writing system consisting of pictures and symbols was created.

The first emperor of China, Huang-ti (ca. 2600 B.C.) ordered one of his talented officials to develop a more simplified writing system. The resulting series of drawings can be regarded as the earliest Chinese characters. These drawings triggered many changes toward simpler forms for easier writing, resulting in a multiform writing system, since each state adopted its own. During the reign of emperor Ch'in Shih-huang (246–214 B.C.), who linked together all sectional walls into what is now known as the Great Wall, one Prime Minister Li-ssu advised the emperor to forbid the use of characters which differed from the ones officially used in the empire. A uniform writing system of drawings was therefore established.

During the same period, however, a prison inspector obtained permission from the emperor to introduce a new and entirely different method using a writing brush, earlier invented by a general named Mêng-t'ien. It was soon widely accepted as the ideal system, because writing with the brush using ink and paper was much faster than writing with the stylus on bamboo or wood. However, the ease with which characters could be written has its drawbacks. It led to alterations of the originals, deviating more and more from the original stylus writings. *Also, because the brush could not make adequate drawings, new drawings were rarely created. New characters were formed consisting of two existing drawings: one gives the general idea of the meaning, the other gives the pronunciation of the character.*

Toward the year 200 A.D., a scholar named Hsü-shên, after long journeys to obtain original stylus writings, wrote a lexicon with short explanatory notes of most characters known at that time. His purpose was to prevent the progressive alteration of the characters, by displaying their authentic forms to all scholars. Called the *Shuo Wên Chieh Tzu* ("On the interpretation of characters") or simply the *Shuo Wên*, it has since been the bible among etymologists.

Why characters are difficult to understand, unless we know their ancestral forms.

The brush writings are only approximations of the stylus drawings, because unlike the stylus, the writing brush cannot make the loops and intricate details that the drawings contain. Also, over the course of time, new types of brush-written characters were introduced by famous scholars. As a result the system has gradually lost its value of being one based on easily understandable drawings, which the old stylus-written system was. On the following pages, examples of the old script are shown which contain excellent information about their meanings, whereas the new script offers little or none whatsoever.

Probably the best examples are given by No.2 and No.3 seen together. The stylus gives an excellent picture of a **Woman** 义 (No.2); by adding two small strokes, the breasts are formed and a picture of **Mother** 义 (No.3) is obtained. The brush-written forms are 女 and 母 : two completely unrelated forms which offer little clue about their meanings.

The stylus gives exquisite portrayals of the **Horse** 馬 (No.4) and the **Bird** 鳥 (No. 5). The brush writings are clumsy, meaningless imitations: 馬 and 鳥 . Nor can the brush draw the pictures for **Music. Joy** 樂 (a musical instrument, No.8) and **Ten thousand** 萬 (a scorpion, No.9), because it cannot draw the small bells and the claws.

Similar remarks can be made with regard to the remaining examples. The stylus drawings reveal the ingenuity and resourcefulness of the ancient Chinese scholars, as can be best be seen in: **Friend** 友 (No.12), **Morning** 朝 (No.13), **West** 西 (No.15), **Gold** 金 (No.16), **Island** 島 (No.17), **Traveler** 旅 (No.19) and **All.The people** 民 (No.20).

The following characters are among the most common and can be seen quite often: 龍 **Dragon** (No.10), **Gold** 金 (No.16), **China** 華 (No.21), **Double joy** 囍 (No.24), **Prosperous** 興 (No.26), **Longevity** 壽 (No.30). None of them contain information about its meaning , which can easily be obtained from its ancestral form.

xii

1		Picture of the heart with the sac opened; the lobes and the aorta are also seen. **Heart**	心
2		Picture of a woman with a curvy figure. **Woman**	女
3		Picture of a woman 女 with breasts added. **Mother**	母
4		Picture of a horse with its mane blowing in the wind. **Horse**	馬
5		Picture of a bird. **Bird**	鳥
6		Picture of a fish: head 𠆢, scaly body ⊖, and tail ⚍. **Fish**	魚
7		Picture of a flying crane. **To fly**	飛
8		A musical instrument: a frame with a drum (in the middle) and bells (on the sides). **Music. Joy**	樂
9		Picture of a scorpion with its head ⊗, legs and tail and its "thousands" of claws. **Ten thousand**	萬
10		A dragon flying toward the sky = and its wings. (It was believed that dragons flew to the sky and produced rain). **Dragon**	龍

xiii

11		An upward-flying bird with wings backward 朩 , trying in vain to reach the sky 一 . **Not. No**	不
12		Two hands working in the same direction. **Friend**	友
13		When the sun ⊝ has risen to the height of a man's helmet ⊕ . **Morning**	早
14		Locks of hair 𝑓 so long that it must be tied with a band – and a brooch 丫 . **Long**	長
15		When birds ⇒ sit on their nests ⊗ , it is evening and the sun is in the West. **West**	西
16		Four nuggets buried (∧ to cover) in the earth ⊥ . **Gold. Metal**	金
17		A mountain ⌣ in the sea, on which birds can rest while crossing it. **Island**	島
18		The sun θ and the sprouting of plants (ψψ plants). **Spring**	春
19		Transients (𝑚 men) seeking shelter under the overhanging branches ∧ of a wind-blown tree . **Traveler**	旅
20		A crowd (人人人 men) as observed by the eye ⊂⊃ . **All. The people**	衆

xiv

21	華	Leaves and flowers 屮屮 that are expanding 于 into full bloom. **China**	華
22	黑	Soot 炏 deposited around the aperture by a smoky fire 炎. **Black**	黑
23	喜	There is singing (ㅂ mouth) and music (hand ⋺ with a stick – beating a drum on a stand 묘). **Joy**	喜
24	囍	Joy 喜 (see No. 23) repeated twice. **Double joy**	囍
25	學	The child 子 in darkness (∩ a small room) and two hands ⌐⌐ of the master pouring knowledge ㄨ . **Learn. Science**	學
26	興	Two pair of hands 𠬞𠬞 lifting up an object harmoniously (∩ cover fits vessel's mouth ㅂ). **Prosperous. Flourishing**	興
27	無	A multitude (ㅡㅡ = ++++ = forty) of men 夳 clearing a forest (many trees 林). **Not. Without**	無
28	食	A pot with contents ㅂ , a ladle 匕 , and the symbol 스 to suggest mixing (three lines coming together). **Food**	食
29	飯	Food 食 (see No. 28) and a hand ⋺ in motion ノ , bringing the food into one's mouth. **Cooked rice. Meal**	飯
30	壽	White hair (hair 屮, change 匕), wrinkles (furrows 乙), to implore (ㅂ mouth, ⋺ hand) for long life. **Longevity**	壽

A Walk through San Francisco's Chinatown

The following pages explain the meanings of commonly seen Chinese characters on the basis of their ancestral forms. San Francisco's Chinatown offers a unique opportunity to study them, because so many characters can be seen inside a relatively small area. Knowing their meanings will allow you to really appreciate their beauty.

It is not necessary for you to do the actual walk.* This chapter and the accompanying photos in the **Photo Section ("Getting to know them"**, starting on page P1) containing multi-choice questions, will give you the means to become quite familiar with them.

---

* For those who only want to acquire a minimum knowledge of 68 characters, there is another book *Read Chinese Today* that I wrote. Containing a Chinatown Map it is specially suitable for those who are in the position of doing the actual walk. (A City Parking Lot is only one block away from the Chinatown Gate, the starting point of the walk.)

I. A Walk through San Francisco's Chinatown.

A short walk through San Francisco's Chinatown will allow us to study and understand common characters. They are very common characters that are used over and over again by the Chinese.

The Entrance Gate to Chinatown bears a sign with a well-known saying by Confucius*: 公 為 下 天 , which written in their ancestral forms would be: 小 爲 丁 夭 . Old Chinese writings are read from right to left**. So the first character is 夭 , which means **HEAVEN** [i.e. *that which expands* ¯ *over* **Man** 大 (*a Man with widespread arms and legs*)]. The second character is 丁 , which means **BELOW** (*an object* | *below a certain level* ¯). The third character was originally written 爲 . It is a picture of a **Female Monkey** with its *claws* 爪 , *body* 广 and *breasts* .. . The original meaning of this character is lost, but one of its present meanings is **FOR** (**For the benefit of**). Lastly, the last character 小 means **COMMON**, or **PUBLIC**. It represents the *division/distribution* 八 *of private property* (厶 *cocoon*, with the self-enclosed silkworm it gives the idea of privacy) *among the common people*. Putting the four meanings together, we would have " Below Heaven For Common". Freely translated it would be: "Under Heaven We All Must Work for the Common Good"(Photo A)

---

* This saying was quoted by **Dr. Sun Yat-Sen** [who led the Revolution that overthrew the Manchu Dynasty (1644-1912)] in one of a series of lectures that he held one year before his death in 1925.

** Writing was done on a roll of paper or silk, with the right hand doing the writing and the left hand holding the roll and unrolling the material. Therefore, writing was done from right to left.

Let us now see characters that we see a lot of times. For instance, we will quite often see these two characters next to each other: 酒家. Originally they were written: 酒家. The first means **Wine** : a *wine jar* and *wine* (*liquid*); the other one means **House(hold)**: a *dwelling* where *pigs* 豕 had free entry ***. The two characters combined mean <u>Wine House</u> or <u>RESTAURANT</u> , namely *one that serves liquor.* **(Photos B,E,G,K).**

The Chinese have other notations for Restaurants. They often use 宮 if it is big and stylish.It means <u>Palace</u> because the original writing is, i.e. a *dwelling* containing a series of (a lot of) rooms . Smaller places quite often call themselves <u>Garden</u> 園 , which was originally written : an *enclosure* , and the symbol inside it, which means *a long robe* * , because the long vines in the garden give the impression as if the trees put on long robes. **(Photo K: Palace),(Photos B,O,M: Garden).**

<u>A bigger restaurant with *dining rooms upstairs,*</u> will use 樓 : a <u>Multi-Story Building</u> . The ancestral form of this character : a building (*tree ,wood*) and (a *woman locked* up in a *lofty palace prison* for misbehavior)**(Photo F).**

Another notation is 飯店; originally written the pair means <u>Rice Shop</u> , because the first is the symbol for **Food** or **Cooked Rice** : a *pot with contents* , a *ladle* and the symbol ∧ - three lines coming together -

---

* The symbol represents the *shoulder* on which the robe rests; the robe is so long that it is *dragging* (a *hook* attached to the harness, used for dragging objects) over the floor.

** This symbol ⊦ represents *cracks* in a tortoise-shell which resulted when it was heated. Divination (fortune-telling) was then spoken out (*mouth*) after closely studying the cracks.

*** To make sure that they were adequately fed.

to suggest *mixing* ; and ┤ is a *hand* in *motion* ⌠ which brings the food into one's mouth. The second character stands for **Shop** (⌠ *shelter* in which *divination* ** 占 is practiced). **(Photo S, in Flower *Shop*.)**

Another combination we'll see is 餐 廳 ., of which the ancestral forms are 飡 廰 . The first character con- sists of many symbols, namely 食 *food* (a *pot with con-tents* ○, a *ladle* ⇦, and ⌒ : three lines coming togeth-er to suggest *mixing*)·; 歺 a *skeleton* after the flesh is re-moved (by a *hand* ㋥). All of them put together they mean **Meal.** How about the other one ? A very complex one , it means **Hall.** It is composed of the symbol ⌠ *shelter* and a very complicated portion 聽 , which means *to hear* and only serves as a "phonetic" (to give the pronunciation of the character). It is used here, because musical performance often takes place here. The two characters combined mean <u>**Meal Hall**</u> , or **Restaurant.** They are often used, because they look very beautiful and distinguished and give a cer-tain dignity to the place. **(Photos H, T, 8)**

Now that we have learned to understand these charac-ters for "Restaurant", can we remember all of them ? The answer should be "Certainly!", especially if we live in San Francisco, because as can be expected, all these characters appear *at the end of the signs* and we can see and recognize them each time we visit Chinatown !

Here are other "pairs" that we can spot easily. Any-where we go, we will find these two together: 公 司 , because they mean <u>**FIRM**</u> or <u>**COMPANY**</u>. In their ances- tral forms they would look like this: 公 司 .The first means **Common:** a *division and distribution* 八 of private prop- erty 厶 (picture of a *cocoon* ; with the self-enclosed silkworm, it gives the idea of 'privacy'). The second symbol 司 is a *man bending over* ㄱ (ㄱ*man) *in order to shout his orders* (ㅂ mouth), and means **To manage**

---

* See Footnote on page W6. ** See Footnote on page W4.

or **Administration**. Combining the two together, we have **Common Administration**. And is this not the idea behind a Firm or Company ? **(Photo I)**

Another pair that we'll see is that which indicates a **BANK.** This pair 銀行 we'll see often enough. It means **Silver Store**, because probably silver was the metal used as currency. (Gold being only used for decorative purposes and in jewelry.) **Silver** was originally written 鑒. It consists of two parts. The first part is 金 *metal***: 金 *four pieces of ore buried* (∧ *cover*) *in the ground*. The other part is 艮 : a *man* 人 * *turning around* 匚 , *in order to look another man 'defiantly' in the eye* 目 . The two parts combined mean **Silver**, because silver is malleable and 'defies' the action of a hammer. **Store** was originally written 行 , to mean *footsteps* ⺀ *made by left* (*and right*) *feet* , and represents "a place where people come and go".
(Photo C: Bank) (Photo U: Herb Store)

Walking through Chinatown, we will occasionally see these three characters next to each other displayed in the window of a restaurant 粥 麵 飯 **(Photo V)**. Written in their ancestral forms they would look like this: 粥 麵 飯. The first one means **PORRIDGE**:*Rice* 米 (*four grains of rice that are scattered* ⺀ *due to thrashing* ┼) *that are thoroughly boiled* (*steam* 弜 *coming from boiling water*). The second character means **NOODLES**. It consists of two portions, of which the second (面 *face*) only serves as a "phonetic", to give the pronunciation of the character. The first portion 麥 means *Wheat* : a plant 止 (picture of a plant with its *trunk* | *branches* ∨ and *roots* ∧) with *ears of grain* 从 ; and 夊 which is a *man* 人 * *who advances* 刀 * *in spite of obstacles* ∧

---

* *The being that has two legs* 人 - only the legs are portrayed. *A man who 'advances'*: a man 人 deformed 刀 , because of his movement. (see last sentence of this page).
** If standing by itself, this symbol means **Gold**.

suggesting the relentless development of the grain. The third character, as we already discussed under "Restaurant", means <u>COOKED RICE</u>.**Having displayed "Porridge, Noodles and Rice (plates)", the place wants to tell the public that it serves all the dishes the public desires, including porridge, which is rarely served in other restaurants.

Another pair of characters that we'll see is that which shows that a restaurant serves **DIM SUM** 點 心 the Cantonese pastry lunch that is very popular in San Francisco, also among tourists **(Photo D).** The original writing would be: 點 心 . The second character is a picture of the **Heart** : it shows the *sac* (opened), the *lobes* and *aorta* . The first character means **Speck** or **Dot**. It consists of two parts: the first part 黑 means black (*soot*) deposited by a *smoky fire* around a *vent*); the second part serves only as a "phonetic", giving an indication how to pronounce the character. The two characters combined mean literally " speck heart ", which freely translated would be "a little heartiness" or simply "a snack" as we say it.

Several times during the walk, we will encounter the character 華 , which stands for <u>CHINA</u> **(Photos B,P,Q).** Originally written 華 , it actually means **Glorious**, being a picture of *a branch with leaves and flowers* expanding * *into full bloom.* It became a symbol for **China**. Usually, however, it is accompanied by another character 中 **Center** (originally : *a target that is pierced in the center by an arrow*), because for the Chinese, China was the center of the World. **(Photos P,Q).**

Often, therefore, we also find the combination 中 國 , which means **Center Country**, to stand for **China**. Originally **Country** was written : a *bordered piece of land*

---

* Breath ╱ after passing an obstacle —, *expanding* freely ⌐ .
** See page W4 (last paragraph).

☐ *defended by weapons (* ⻊ *halberd) with a capital* ○.
(Photos C,U)

Now that we know how the Chinese write "China", we would like to know how they write **AMERICA** ! We see it on the sign for the Bank of America: 美國銀行.
(Photo C)   The last two characters mean **Bank**,we know from the above.** The second character we just met: **Country**. The first 美 means **Beautiful**. Originally written 美 , it is composed of *sheep* 羊 (picture of a sheep,seen from behind, showing the *horns* 丫 , *four feet and tail* ⟂) and *big* 大 (a man with outstretched arms, as if he wants to show how big something is), to give the meaning **Beautiful**(*a big sheep being a beautiful animal*). Combining the two characters together we get **Beautiful Country**.

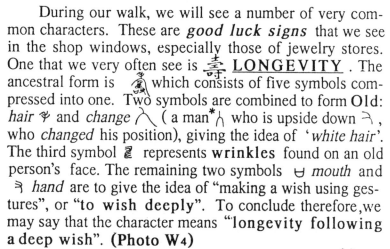

During our walk, we will see a number of very common characters. These are *good luck signs* that we see in the shop windows, especially those of jewelry stores. One that we very often see is 壽 **LONGEVITY** . The ancestral form is 𦉢 which consists of five symbols compressed into one. Two symbols are combined to form **Old**: *hair* 屮 and *change* 𠤎 (a man* 𠤎 who is upside down 𠃑 , who *changed* his position), giving the idea of '*white hair*'. The third symbol 彡 represents **wrinkles** found on an old person's face. The remaining two symbols 𠙵 *mouth* and 彐 *hand* are to give the idea of "making a wish using gestures", or "**to wish deeply**". To conclude therefore,we may say that the character means "**longevity following a deep wish**". **(Photo W4)**

Another character that we'll meet quite often is 囍. It means **DOUBLE JOY** and is usually used to celebrate a wedding. Invitation cards for the wedding are printed with this character, many times in gold. It is the character for **JOY** 喜 repeated twice, or 𠧢 in its original form, which indicates that there is *singing* (𠙵

---

* See page W6 (Footnote).   ** See page W6.

mouth) and *music* (a *hand* ⟋ with a *stick* — beating a *drum on a stand* 且). (**Photos W3** and **W8**, where it appears on a jar and a flower pot, respectively.)

The good luck sign that can appear on almost any article is 福 for **HAPPINESS**. (**Photos W1, W5, W4** where it appears on an emblem, a kimono, a statue representing a happy father blessed with a son.) We can explain its meaning by looking at the original form 福 . The left-hand part represents a *heavenly sign* (= *heaven*, and ∥ *what comes down from heaven*) *that brings prosperity*; the right-hand part shows *products* ○ *from the field* ⊕ *being under one's roof* ⌃ .

As can be expected, the character 愛 for **LOVE** is very popular and very common. (See **Photo W2** where it appears on a child's dress .) Looking at its ancestral form 愛 we can see the symbol for **Heart** ⼼ that we met before (in **Photo D**): it is a picture of the heart, showing the *sac* (opened), the *lobes* and the *aorta*. Combined with 旡 **To swallow** (a *man* ⼍ *breathing in air* =), it means: **to swallow affectionate feelings down in one's heart.** The other symbol 夊 (a *man* 刀 *who advances in spite of obstacles* ⌒) is added to indicate that it is a **lingering feeling.**

Two animals that the Chinese like to use to name their businesses are the **HORSE** 馬 and the **DRAGON** 龍. The original script for the Horse is 馬 , which is a clever picture of the animal, with its mane blowing in the wind. The original form for the Dragon is 龍 . It shows on the left-hand side *the animal* ⾉ *flying towards the sky* = , and on the right-hand side its *wings* ⼃ . The Chinese namely believed that dragons could fly towards the sky and thereby produce rain. As a rule, we find "golden" added as an adjective so that during our walk we'll find "Golden Dragon" as the name for a restaurant (**G**). The character

---

* See page W6 (Footnote).

for <u>GOLD</u> is 金, or 金 in its original form. It shows *four gold nuggets* 金 *buried (∧ cover) in the ground* *. For Horse, the adjective <u>PRECIOUS</u> 寶 is also used. The ancestral form shows *three precious possessions found in one's house* 寶 : *jade* 王 , *porcelain (⊕ earthenware) and money (* 貝 *shell*, formerly used as money *)*. **(Photo G – Gold) (Photo T – Precious)**

Let us now take a look at a series of characters that are commonly used by the Chinese, because they deal with the good things in life.

The character for <u>JOY</u> is 喜. We met this before in <u>DOUBLE JOY</u> **(Photo W3, W6)** Written 喜 it means: *there is music (a hand* ⇒ *with a stick* ― *beating a drum on a stand* 豆 *) and singing (* 口 *mouth)*. **(Photo I)** Repeated twice, it is used during wedding celebrations because it is indeed a joyful event for both wife and husband.

貴 Two other common characters 富 <u>WEALTHY</u> and 貴 <u>PRECIOUS, HONORABLE</u> appear next to each other on a sign for a flower shop. The first was originally written 富 and means: *having products* ○ *of the field* ⊕ *stacked up* ∧ *under one's roof* ∧ . The second was 貴 and means: *a basket* 虫 *containing money (* 貝 *shell*, formerly used as money), or in other words 'something precious'. **(Photo S)**

---

* If used as a component in a character, it means **Metal** (*four pieces of metal ore buried in the ground*). See, e.g. **Silver**, previously discussed under <u>BANK</u>. (See page **W6**)

The next character, 香 means **FRAGRANT** and is closely linked with 港**HARBOR**, because the two combined mean **HONG KONG**. The original writing for **FRAGRANT** was 香 , meaning *the sweet* 甘 (*the mouth* 口 *holding something – agreeable) odor of grain* 禾 (*a plant* 禾 *with ripening ears at the top* 丿) *that is fermenting (* 丷 *vapors).* The old writing for **HARBOR** was 巷, meaning: *water* 水 *and* 巷 *what is commonly used (* 廿 = ++ = *twenty,* 廾 *pair of hands) in the city* 邑 *(a city* ○ *and its seal* 阝). **(Photo N)**

And finally, one character with a very positive tone: **PEACE** 平, which was originally written 平 , meaning *the breath* 丂 *going through an obstacle* — *and spreading out freely and evenly* 兀 . **(Photo M)**

Many times, two or more characters combine to form one meaning(as we have seen earlier with **RESTAU-RANT**, **BANK**, **FIRM**). Here are more examples that we'll meet:

SEAFOOD 海鮮 which is 海 Sea (see p.**W14**) and 鮮 **Fresh** [namely, 魚(**Fish** , picture of a Fish) and 羊 (**Sheep****), which were eaten raw by the ancient Chinese, and therefore had to be fresh].

WORLD 世界, which is **Generation** 世 (*three times ten* +, which was apparently man's life expectancy at that time) and **Boundary** 界 (*land (* ⊕ *field) and separation* 八 *of men* 丿). **(Photos D,R)**

ASIA 亞 洲 , which is 亞 (pronounced *Y a*, it is used for its pronunciation only), and **Continent** 洲 (*water* 水 *and tracts of land through which rivers flow* 州). **(Photo O)**

---

* It is *man* 人 (**W6**, Footnote) in a bent position 丿 .

** Picture of a sheep (seen from behind), with its *horns* 丫, *four feet and tail* ‡ .

<u>NEWSPAPER</u>日報, which is **Sun, Day** ⊙ (picture of the *sun*) and **Announcement, Newspaper** 報 : *a criminal* (辛 * *to offend, commit crime against man* 人) *and a hand* 又 *holding a seal* 卩 : *an official announcement (of a judgement).* **(Photo R)**

<u>TRADE CENTER</u> 商 塲. In its original form **Trade** 商 looks like a picture of a human face. But actually it consists of three portions: 言 <u>words</u> (*the tongue* 舌 *shown outside the mouth, and* = *the sound produced by it* ; <u>within</u> (*an object* 入 *entering a certain space* 冂); *and* <u>two suns</u> ⊙⊙ (*picture of two suns*). The three portions put together mean *when words are spoken inside a room, lasting several days* : **Trade**. The second character actually means **Arena**, or **Open space**. It was formerly written 塲 and means: *land* (土 ** *earth*) *and* (*the sun* ⊖ *rising* ∧ *above the horizon* — *and its rays* � *shining over an open space*). **(Photo N)**

<u>ASSOCIATION</u> 會 館 . The first character means **Society**, earlier written as :*meeting* (∧ *three lines coming together*) *and words* (*that* ⌐ *which comes out from the mouth* ⊔) *are spoken at the fireside* (*smoke outlet*) . The second character means **Restaurant**, or **Hall**, formerly written 館 : *a large building* (*building* ∩ *with many steps*), *where food* (*a pot with contents* ⊖ , *a ladle* , *and the symbol* ∧ *to suggest 'mixing'* (*three lines coming together*) *is served*. **(Photo P)**

---

* The symbol 辛 represents a *pestle*, capable of producing a grinding, unpleasant action.

** The layer = from which all things | come out.

Four characters are very common, i.e. 北 NORTH, 南 SOUTH, 東 EAST, and 西 WEST. We can easily derive their meanings from their ancestral forms. NORTH)|(: *two men turning their backs towards the North.* (Facing the South was a Chinese custom during ceremonies.) SOUTH 凷 : *the area 冫 冫 where vegetation (ψ plant) expands continuously (丰 a pestle; the additional stroke — suggests the idea of repetition or continuity).* EAST 東 : *the sun 田 is in the East when it is so low that we can see it shining behind the trees 木 (of the Eastern mountains). · WEST 棲 : when birds 乌 sit on their nests 田 it is evening and the sun is in the West.* (Photo U: South, North)

During our walk we'll pass the sign "Four Seas". So let us now disscuss characters which mean numbers. The Chinese have very simple symbols for the numbers ONE, TWO, and THREE , which are represented by *one stroke* — (一), *two strokes* 二 (二), and *three strokes* 三 (三). The numbers Four, Six and Eight are given symbols which convey the idea that they are 'even' numbers. FOUR ⑰ *means a quantity that can be divided into two equal portions* (now written 四). (Photo E) SIX ⑰ is the same symbol, but *with a dot added to distinguish it from Four.* The modern brush-written form is 六. EIGHT was the simple symbol)((now written 八), meaning *a quantity consisting of two equal halves.* TEN was a *cross* 十 (now written 十), an appropriate symbol, because Ten is a unit. FIVE is also a unit in China (e.g., as used in the abacus), since we have five fingers on each hand. The old symbol was a *diagonal cross* X , now 五. SEVEN is a unit used in fortune-telling and was written 十 : *a cross with a "tail" to distinguish it from the unit Ten.* It is now written 七 . (Photo I) And finally, NINE 九, almost the unit Ten, formerly written 九 : a "wavy" 十 (Ten).

北

南

東

西

一

二

三

四

六

八

十

五

七

九

To end our discussion, let us now take a look at a few more common characters. **RULER**, or **EMPRESS** 后 * (*see* **Photo F**) formerly written represents a *man bending over* *to give orders* (𝕌 *mouth*) *to the people.*
FLOWER 花 (*see* **Photo S**) formerly written   means: *that portion of plants* ΨΨ *that has greatly changed* (*a man* 𝕀 * and 𝕌 a man-upside-down: a man who 'changed' his position*). **HERBS**, or **MEDICINE** 藥 **(Photo U)** , formerly written consists of two parts. The first part, the one on top, is the symbol for **grass***ΨΨ. The second part looks very complicated, but it is simply a picture of a musical instrument (*a frame with a drum in the middle and bells on the sides*) and represents **Music**, or **Joy**. The two parts put together mean: *herbs (grass) that restore harmony (music, joy) in our body.* **SEA** 海 (*see* **(Photo E)** was formerly written . This symbol consists of three parts. One part is **Water** put on the left-hand side. The second part is **Mother** (*picture of a woman with prominent breasts*). The third part is **Grass** Ψ, to give the idea of abundance. The three parts put together mean: *the source of all waters*. **PASTRY**, **CAKES** 餅 (*see* **Photo M**), formerly written has on the left-hand side the symbol for **Food** that we have encountered many times (see pp. **W4**, **W5**, **W12**) . It represents *a pot with contents* ⊖ , *a ladle* ⟨ , *and the symbol* △ *to suggest 'mixing'* (*three lines coming together).* The right-hand part means **Harmony**: *two men* 𝝸 *marching in step* == . **TO LEARN** 學 (*see* **Photo Q**), formerly written represents *a child* 𝔖 *in darkness* ⌒ (*a small room)* *and two hands* ⴹⵑ *of the master pouring down knowledge* ᚛

**As a rule, symbols dealing with vegetative material have the symbol for *grass* ΨΨ added on top.

* See page W6 (Footnote).

Common Characters in Chinatown (1)

Character & Meaning *	References to Photos **
四 Four[4]	E (Four Seas). 12
七 Seven[7]	I (Chat Hai)
心 Heart[21]	D (World Pastry). L. 2. 23
后 Empress[46]	F (Empress China)
馬 Horse[54]	T (Young's Cafe). 31
龍 Dragon[61]	G (Golden Dragon). 31
花 Flower[68]	S (May's Flowers).
藥 Herbs[72]	U (China Herbs). 7
日 Sun[73]	R (World Journal)
天 Heaven[76]	A (Chinatown Gate)
山 Mountain[86]	4 (Chinese Times). 19
海 Sea[92]	E (Four Seas). T
洲 Continent[94]	O (Asia Garden). 16
金 Gold[96]	G (Golden Dragon)
銀 Silver[97]	C (Bank America)
餐 Meal[104]	H. T (Young's Cafe). 8
飯 Rice[105]	H. L. V. 12 (Szechuan)
粥 Porridge[107]	H. V (Tong Kee)
麵 Noodles[108]	H. V (Tong Kee)
餅 Pastry[112]	M (Ping Yuen)

* Numbers refer to the Dictionary for its etymology.
** The ones with their names are the most illustrative.
Circle the ones that you know already !

Common Characters in Chinatown (2)

Character & Meaning *	References to Photos **
酒 Wine[115] 報 Newspaper[134] 司 Management[139] 商 Trade[153] 行 Store[157]	B. E. F. G. K. 1. 6, etc. R (World Journal). 4. 19 I (Chat Hai). 5. 10. 11 N (Hong Kong). 9. 23 C. U. 7. 16. 22 (Bank)
店 Shop[158] 家 Household[162] 廳 Hall[165] 園 Garden[166] 樓 Story-house[167]	L. S. 12. 13. 17. 32, etc. B. E. G. K. M. 1. 6, etc. H. T. 8 (Ping's Place) B. M (Ping Yuen). O F. 14 (Ming Palace)
宮 Palace[168] 館 Hall[170] 會 Society[172] 國 Country[174] 塲 Arena[175]	K (Imperial Palace). 14 P (Chinese Association) P (Chinese Association). 9. 15 C (Bank America). U. 23 N (Hong Kong)
港 Harbor[177] 華 China[180] 中 Center[196] 下 Below[198] 北 North[200]	N (Hong Kong) B. P. Q. 7. 9. 18 P. Q. U. 7. 9. 22. 23 A (Chinatown Gate) U (China Herbs)

* Numbers refer to the Dictionary for its etymology.
** The ones with their names are the most illustrative.
Circle the ones that you know already !

Common Characters in Chinatown (3)

Character & Meaning *	References to Photos **
南 South[201]	U (China Herbs)
大 Big[208]	G (Golden Dragon).10. 21
美 Beautiful[218]	C (Bank America)
香 Fragrant[221]	N (Hong Kong). 6
貴 Honorable[229]	S (May's Flowers)
寶 Precious[230]	T (Young's Cafe). 16
公 Common[234]	A. I (Chat Hai). 5. 10. 11
亞 Ya (Second)[236]	O. 16 (Asia Jewelry)
世 Generation[246]	D. R (World Journal). 2
界 Border[247]	D. R (World Journal). 2
平 Peace[248]	M (Ping Yuen). 17
喜 Joy[256]	I (Chat Hai). 20
富 Wealthy[258]	S (May's Flowers)
福 Happiness[259]	W1. W4. W5 (in windows)
愛 Love[262]	W2 (in windows)
壽 Longevity[264]	W4 (in windows)
囍 Double Joy[268]	W3 (in windows)
財 Wealth[269]	20 (Gung Hay Fat Choy)
學 Learn[272]	Q (Chinese School)
點 Speck[283]	D (World of Patry)

* Numbers refer to the Dictionary for its etymology.
** The ones with their names are the most illustrative.
Circle the ones that you know already !

> *To learn and at due times to repeat what one has learned, is that not, after all, a pleasure ?* **Confucius**

Getting to Know Them – Photo Section

In my other book, *Read Chinese Today*, you became familiar with the 68 most commonly seen characters through questions (and answers) during a walk* through San Francisco's Chinatown. This book will help you to increase your knowledge to 288 common characters.

Before we do this, however, we should refresh our knowledge of the 68 characters, by completing the multi-choice questions that go with the Photos A to W.

This section also contains text which introduces **new characters** in the same format that was followed in the "Chinatown Walk" chapter.

In **How to Use the Character Finder and to Find a Character in this Book** (pages P34-35), you will find instructions for writing Chinese characters. This allows you to find the number of strokes in a character, which then allows you to find the meaning and explanation of the character through the **Character Finder** *(shaded pages A to F before the Dictionary).*

* Imaginary or actual walk.

Practice Page
Write the correct letters on the dotted lines.

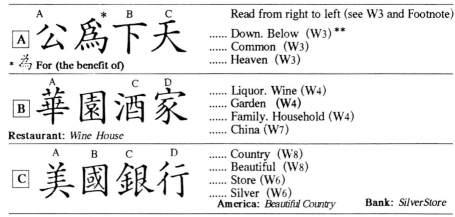

Read from right to left (see W3 and Footnote)

A 公 爲* 下 天
  A   B   C
* 爲 **For (the benefit of)**

...... Down. Below (W3) **
...... Common (W3)
...... Heaven (W3)

B 華 園 酒 家
  A   C   D
Restaurant: *Wine House*

...... Liquor. Wine (W4)
...... Garden (W4)
...... Family. Household (W4)
...... China (W7)

C 美 國 銀 行
  A   B   C   D

...... Country (W8)
...... Beautiful (W8)
...... Store (W6)
...... Silver (W6)
America: *Beautiful Country*   **Bank:** *SilverStore*

** W3, etc. refer to pages W3, etc. of the "Chinatown Walk" chapter.

The character for **Heaven** *(in A)* is a very simple one, and so is the one for **Earth** 土, formerly written 圭 : the layer 二 from which all things | come out.

土

As we have seen, the symbol for **Down** or **Below** *(in A)* is of utmost simplicity. As can be expected, the one for **Up** or **Above** is ⊥ *(an object | above a certain level —)*, now written as 上 . 上海 [W14] is "**Shanghai**" *(above the sea)*.

上

The character **Common** *(in A)* can be seen many times, because combined with **Management** 司 (W5) it means **FIRM** or **COMPANY**, as we have seen (W5).

Garden *(in B)* stands for **RESTAURANT,** as well as other characters mentioned on W4 and W5. Another one is 廚, formerly 廚 : *a sheltered place* 广 : *where one pre-pares one's meal* 豆 * *(hand* ⇒ *, and* ⇒ *a hand that measures* < – *measuring stick* > *)*, normally used by smaller restaurants. Also used for a small restaurant is 室, formerly 室 , which means **Room**: *a dwelling* 宀 *to which one returns after work (a bird* 至 *with wings backward, coming down to earth* 土 [85]*)*.** Also 屋 or 室 means **Room.** The bottom portion is the same as the one just discussed; the top portion means: *a man in a sitting, or resting position.*

廚

室

屋

* A simple meal (• bean) served on a stemmed platter. Also the symbol for **Bean**[109]   ** Refers to Character No. 85 in the Dictionary.

Practice Page
Write the correct letters on the dotted lines.

D	A 點	B 心	C 世	D 界

...... Border. Boundary (W11)
...... Heart (W7)
...... Speck. Dot (W7)
.... Generation. World (W11)

Dim Sum: *Speck Heart (a little heartiness).* **World:** *Generation Boundary*

E	A 四	B 海	C 酒	D 家

...... Sea (W14)
...... Four (W13)
...... Family. Household (W4)
...... Wine. Liquor (W4)

Restaurant: *Wine House*

F	A 皇	B 后	C 酒	D 樓

...... Multi-story house (W4)
...... Empress (D46*)
...... Wine. Liquor (W4)

Sovereign

G	A 金	B 龍	C 大	D 酒	E 家

...... Wine. Liquor (W4)
...... Dragon (W9)
...... Family. Household (W4)
...... Gold (W10)
...... Big. Great (D208)

* D46 = Dictionary, Character No. 46.

Sea 海 *(Photo E)* can be seen quite often, because combined with **Fresh** 鮮 (W11) they mean "**Seafood**" (W11, *Photo T*). 洋 **Ocean**, formerly 洋 *(water ⸬ and* 羊 *as "phonetic"),* can be found in 太平洋 "**Pacific Ocean**" (Very* Peaceful[W11] Ocean).   Many other characters relating to *NATURE* are also commonly used by the Chinese.

Stream or **River** 川 *(⫶⫶* *a big stream formed by smaller streams)* can be seen combined with **Four** 四 (W13) ,because the two mean "**Szechwan**"(the "four rivers province"), a province known also for its cuisine *(Photo12).* Another writing for **River** is 河 *(*河 *: water ⸬ and* 可 *as "phonetic").* The "**Yellow River**" is 黄[102] 河 *(Huang Ho).*

Mountain 山 *(⛰ picture of a mountain)* is seen many times in San Francisco, because 金山 (Gold [W10] Mountain) means "**San Francisco** *(Photos 4 and 19).*

Very 太 *(*大[208] **Big** with a *dot* added: " *very* big".

點心世界
WORLD OF PASTRY

RESTAURANT

CHINESE LUNCH 中國
PEKING CUISINE 早點

D

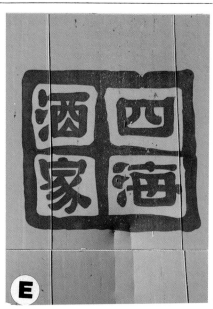

四海
酒家

E

皇后酒樓
EMPRESS OF CHINA
ROOF GARDEN RESTAURANT · COCKTAILS

F

GOLDEN DRAGON

金龍大酒家

DINING
COCKTAILS

RESTAURANT

G

Practice Page
Write the correct letters or correct meaning on the dotted lines.

粥 　 麵 　 飯

.... (W6) 　 .... (W6) 　 .... (W7)

H

A　*　B　C
長 城 餐 廳

...... Hall (W5)
...... Meal. Food (W5)
...... Long (D212)**

Great Wall: *Long *City Wall* 　 **Restaurant:** *Meal Hall*

I

A　B　C　D
七 喜 公 司

...... Common (W5)
...... Seven (W13)
...... Management (W5)
...... Joy (W8)

Company: *Common Management*

J

興 興 　 .... (D267)**

K

*　A　B　C
皇 宮 酒 家

...... Wine. Liquor (W4)
...... House (W4)
...... Palace (W4)

* Imperial 　 **Restaurant:** *Wine House*

** D212, D267, etc. means: Dictionary, Character Nos. 212, 267, etc.

We met **Sun** or **Day** 日 ^W12 in "Daily Newspaper" *(Photo R)*.
Moon 月 (𝒟 *is a picture of a crescent moon)*. It also means
Month, so that 一 月 means **"January"** *(month one* ^W13*)*.
The character for **Star** is 星 : *sublimed matter ascending*
∨ *from the earth* 土 ^85 *to become stars* ∘°∘ : 壆 · *(Photo 5)*.

Water 水 (⺡ *picture of a small stream* ＼ *with whirls
of water* ⺡ . It can be found in its condensed form 氵 in
characters that represent items of liquid or watery nature. (See,
for example, 酒 **Wine**^W4, 海 **Sea**^W14 and 洋 **Ocean**, 河
River, both discussed on previous page. Also in **Lake** 湖
(*Water* ⺡ *and* 古月 *as "phonetic")*, which can be seen often,
because 湖 南 ^W13 *(South Lake)* means **"Hunan"**, as in
"Hunan Restaurant".

月

星

水

湖

H

I

J

K

P8

Practice Page
Write the correct letters on the dotted lines.

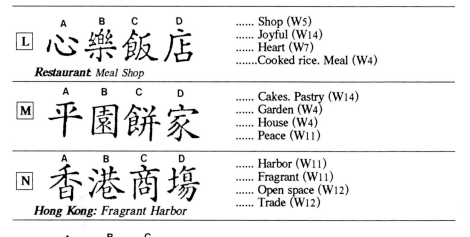

心樂飯店
Restaurant: Meal Shop

...... Shop (W5)
...... Joyful (W14)
...... Heart (W7)
.......Cooked rice. Meal (W4)

M 平園餅家

...... Cakes. Pastry (W14)
...... Garden (W4)
...... House (W4)
...... Peace (W11)

N 香港商塲
Hong Kong: Fragrant Harbor

...... Harbor (W11)
...... Fragrant (W11)
...... Open space (W12)
...... Trade (W12)

O 亞洲園

...... Garden (W4)
...... *Ya* (W11) *
...... Continent (W11)

* As a rule, this character is only used as a phonetic *(Ya)*. e.g. in 亞洲亞*(Ya Chou Ya)* to indicate "Asia".

The symbol for **Fire** was *a pile of wood burning with flames:* 兆 , now written 火 . **Light** was 光 :*a torch (火 fire) carried by a man* 允 *(but only his legs are shown),* now written 光. **Shadow** 影 was 影: *shadows ⁄ caused by bright light (the sun* W12 ⊙ *high* 高 *< picture of a tower> up in the sky).* When combined with 電 (**Electricity,** *see below),* it means **"Film", "Motion Picture"** 電影 (electric shadow). **Rain** was 雨 : *drops of water ⌶ falling down | from clouds* ∩ *suspended from the sky* ⌐, now written 雨 . **Lightning** or **Electricity** was 電: *that which extends* ⴹ *from the rain* 雨 *and strikes down* ㇠, now written 電. It is a very common character, because with 話**Talk, Speech** (話*the tongue* 舌 *and words* ⌇ *coming from the tongue* 舌) it means **"Telephone"** 電話 *(Photo 24).*

心樂飯店
SAM LOK
RESTAURANT

PING YUEN
RESTAURANT

香港商場
HONG
KONG
CENTER

Practice Page
Write the correct letters on the dotted lines.

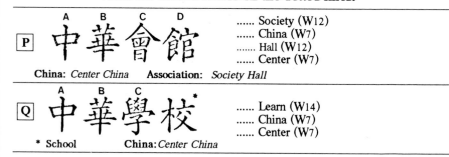

P 中華會館

A B C D

...... Society (W12)
...... China (W7)
.... Hall (W12)
...... Center (W7)

China: *Center China*   Association: *Society Hall*

Q 中華學校

A B C *

...... Learn (W14)
...... China (W7)
...... Center (W7)

* School   China: *Center China*

Cloud 雲 was formerly written 雲, meaning: *vapors*
∨ *rising to the skies* = *and producing rain* 霝 *(see P8 last par.)*. Combined with 吞 **To gulp down** (吞 *to swallow*
< 口 *mouth* > *in one* − *big* 大 < *a person with outstretched arms, as if showing the size of a large object* > *effort)*, the pair means **"Wonton"**, as in "Wonton soup" that popular Chinese dish ("that cloudy delicacy that one gulps down"!).

Wind was 風 (*insect* 虫 < *picture of an insect* > *and air in motion* 凡). *It was believed that insects were born when the wind blew.* Now written 風 it occurred in combination with 東 **East**[W13] to form "Eastwind" 東風, as in "Eastwind Books and Arts"*(Photo 32).*

Two characters that mean the source of water are: **Spring** or **Fountain** 泉 (泉 *water spouting up* T *and expanding evenly* 水) and **Spring** or **Source** 源 (源 *water* 水 *and fountain* 泉 < *see previous character* > *coming out from the cliff* 厂)*.* The second character has the condensed form of **Water** 氵 built in it. (See also in **Wine** (W4) and **Sea** (W14)).

Finally, under the group **NATURE**, we have **Island** 島 (島 *a mountain* 山 < *picture of a mountain* > *in the sea, on which birds* 鳥 *can rest while crossing)*.

Practice Page
Write the correct letters on the dotted lines.

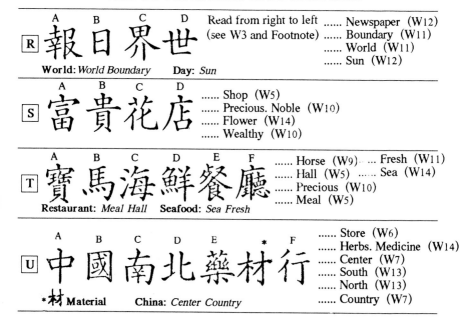

	A	B	C	D		
R	報	日	界	世	Read from right to left ...... Newspaper (W12)
					(see W3 and Footnote) ...... Boundary (W11)
					...... World (W11)
					...... Sun (W12)

World: *World Boundary* **Day:** *Sun*

	A	B	C	D
S	富	貴	花	店

...... Shop (W5)
...... Precious. Noble (W10)
...... Flower (W14)
...... Wealthy (W10)

	A	B	C	D	E	F
T	寶	馬	海	鮮	餐	廳

...... Horse (W9) ... Fresh (W11)
...... Hall (W5) ...... Sea (W14)
...... Precious (W10)
...... Meal (W5)

Restaurant: *Meal Hall* **Seafood:** *Sea Fresh*

	A	B	C	D	E	*	F
U	中	國	南	北	藥	材	行

...... Store (W6)
...... Herbs. Medicine (W14)
...... Center (W7)
...... South (W13)
...... North (W13)
...... Country (W7)

***材 Material**   **China:** *Center Country*

Other very common characters are 好 <u>Good</u>, <u>Fine</u> [㕚 , which is: *to have a wife* 㞢 *and child(ren)* 㝂 *(Photo 13)*] and <u>Bright</u> 明 [㊊㋐ *the moon* 㝱 < *picture of a crescent moon* > *shines through the window* 㡳 *and the room is brightly lit*] *(Photo 14)*.　　好　明

<u>Capital</u> 京 was written 京, which is *a picture of a city-tower*. It can be seen quite often, because 北^W13 京 stands for "Beijing" ("*northern capital*", as opposed to "Nanjing" 南^W13 京 ("*southern capital*").　京

Two characters are common and often seen. They are 女, which was 㞢 : *a picture of a woman with a curvy figure* and 男, which was 㽞 *the one that gives his strength* < 㗊 *picture of a muscle in its sheath* > *in the field* 㽀 . They mean <u>Woman</u> (<u>Female</u>) and <u>Man</u> (<u>Male</u>) and are important, because they indicate restroom facilities, and they may not always be translated for you! *(Photo 33)*　女　男

世界日報
WORLD JOURNAL

824
世界書局

R

貴富
店花

872

S

名廚泡製
LUNCH · DINNER
FOOD TO GO 397-3455

寶馬海鮮餐廳

與泉不

YOUNG'S CAFE

AUTHENTIC
CHINESE CUIS

Budweiser

OPEN

Young's Cafe

MORE SEATIN
DOWNSTAIR
LARGE DIN

T

中國南北藥材行

CHINA HERBS

時式
髮型

DAVID'S
HAIR
DESIGN

CHINA HERBS

U

Practice Page
Write the correct letters on the dotted lines.

V   ^A粥   ^B麵   ^C飯   ...... Rice (plates) (W7)
                                     ...... Noodles (W6)
                                     .... Porridge (W6)

W   ^A福   ^B愛   ^C囍   ...... Double joy (W8)
                                     ...... Happiness. Good fortune (W9)
                                     ...... Love (W9)

Here are more characters that are Good Luck Signs.
Wealth 財 *(貝⼓ shows a hand ⼓ that has just brought in money < 貝 a shell, formerly used as money >).* You can see this character in 恭喜發財, meaning "Happy New Year!" *(Wishing [287] you joy [256] and expanding [288] wealth [269]!)* *(Photo 20).*

Another one that we see quite often is 安, which means **Peaceful**, **Secure** *(房\ a woman 女 secure within the confines of the house ⼧).*

Having our meal in a Chinese restaurant, the waitress will sometimes serve us tea in a teapot with the following inscription 如意吉祥 *(Photo 25).* It means " **According to** one's **Wishes**(意 *expressing one's deep wishes < 心 heart > through one's words 言, the tongue 舌 and = the sound produced by it)* :to be **Lucky** (吉 *achieving good fortune, as foretold < 口 mouth > by a sage < 士 one who has knowledge of all things (between the two units "one"— and "ten" +)>)* and **Happy**(示羊 *sign coming down ⼩ from heaven = proclaiming peace < 羊 sheep[50] >)* "

The ancient symbol for **Joy** or **Joyful** is *a picture of a musical instrument* 樂 *(a wooden frame with a drum in the middle and bells on the sides).* Nowadays it is written as 樂 *(Photo L).* When the symbol for **Grass** 艹 is put on top, the character means **Medicinal herbs** or **Medicine**, i.e. herbs that restore harmony ("Joy") *(Photo U).*

V

W₁

W₂

W₃

Practice Page
Write the correct letters or correct meanings on the dotted lines.

W4	A 壽	B 祥	C 福	...... Happiness (W9) ...... Lucky(D257) ...... Longevity (W8)

| W5 | 福 | .... (W9) |

| W6 | 囍 | .... (W8) |

Here follow other characters that are grouped under the Good Luck Signs in the Dictionary.

誠 (誠 *to accomplish* 成 < *a boy* 人 *that has reached man-hood and can handle the sword* 戈 > *what one has promised* < 言 *273 words* >): <u>Sincere</u>. <u>Honest</u>. *(Photo 3)*. 誠

The symbol for <u>**To prosper**</u> was 興 , which represents *two pair of hands* 臼 廾 *lifting up an object in a harmonious way* (同 *agreement: a cover* 冂 *that perfectly fits a vessel's mouth* 口). The modern writing is 興 *(Photo 3)*. 興

The character 和 means <u>**Harmonious**</u>, which was written 禾口, *because it is only natural ("harmonious") for grain* 禾 *(a plant* 木 *with ripening ears hanging down at the top* 丿) *to be consumed (* 口 *mouth) (Photo 11)*. 和

The character for <u>**Good**</u>, <u>**Kind**</u>, <u>**Friendly**</u> is 善 . The an-cient writing was 譱 : *dispute (* 言 *273 words, repeated)* *peacefully (* 羊 *50 sheep) settled and harmony restored.* 善

Another one commonly seen is 昌 : <u>**Prosperous**</u>, <u>**Flour-ishing**</u>. The ancient form showed *the sun* 日 *and the moon* 月 *(a crescent moon) shining at the same time* 昌 . 昌

As can be expected, some of these characters above are used for names under the assumption that they bring good luck.

Longevity 壽　Prosperity 祿　Happiness 福

Fine ·PEKING· Cloisonneware

W4

W5

W6

Practice Page
Write the correct character numbers on the dotted lines.

1 金⁹⁶ 鳳* 酒¹¹⁵ 家¹⁶²
...... Home. House
...... Gold
...... Wine

Restaurant: *Wine House* ***鳳 Phoenix**

---

2 世²⁴⁵ 界²⁴⁷ 人³² 參* 中¹⁹⁵ 心²¹
...... Center
...... Boundary
...... World
...... Heart

Center: *Center Heart*
* Ginseng: 人參 *(used here as phonetics).* **World:** *World Boundary*

---

3 誠²⁵⁵ 興²⁶⁷
...... Sincere. Honest
...... To prosper

NOTE: Superscript numbers above characters refer to Character Numbers in the Dictionary.

---

4 金⁹⁶ 山⁸⁶ 時¹⁸¹ 報¹³⁴
...... Newspaper
...... Gold
...... Time
...... Mountain

San Francisco: *Gold Mountain*

---

5 星⁷⁵ 河⁰⁸ 視* 聽* 公²³⁴ 司¹³⁹
... Common
... Star
...... Administration
...... River

* 視 See * 聽 Hear. Rainbow: *Star River*
Company: *Common Administration*

---

6 一¹ 品¹²⁹ 香²²¹ 酒¹¹⁵ 家¹⁶²
...... House
...... Fragrant
...... One
...... Product

Restaurant: *Wine House*

---

7 萬¹³ 華¹⁸⁰ 中¹⁹⁶ 藥⁷² 行¹⁵⁷
...... Store
...... Ten thousand
...... Center
...... China
...... Herbs. Medicine

All Chinese: *Ten-thousand Chinese*

Practice Page

Write the correct character numbers on the dotted lines.

---

8 紅 棉 餐 廳
100 71 104 165

...... Hall
...... Red
...... Cotton
...... Meal

Restaurant: *Meal Hall*

---

9 中 華 總 商 會
196 180 x 153 172

...... Association
...... Center
...... China
...... Trade

* **Main. General**   **China:** *Center China*

---

10 大 方 農 產 公 司
208 233 152 151 204 139

...... Administration
...... Big
...... To produce
...... Agriculture
...... Square
...... Common

Company: *Common Administration*

---

11 兆 和 肉 食 公 司
* 249 110 103 234 139

...... Common
...... Harmony
...... Meat
...... Administration
...... Food

* 兆 **Million**   **Company:** *Common Administration*

---

12 四 川 飯 店
4 87 105 158

...... Shop
...... Stream
...... Meal
...... Four

Szechwan: *Four Streams*   **Restaurant:** *Rice Shop*

---

13 好 好 糕 粉 店
215 215 113 111 158

...... Shop
...... Good
...... Flour
...... Pastry

---

14 明 宮 酒 樓
217 168 115 167

...... Liquor. Wine
...... Palace
...... Multi-story house
...... Bright

Practice Page

Write the correct character numbers on the dotted lines.

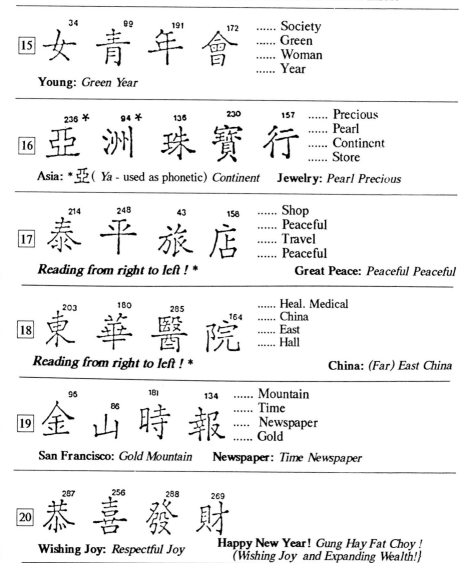

15 女(34) 青(89) 年(191) 會(172)

...... Society
...... Green
...... Woman
...... Year

Young: *Green Year*

---

16 亞(236)* 洲(94)* 珠(136) 寶(230) 行(157)

...... Precious
...... Pearl
...... Continent
...... Store

Asia: *亞(Ya - used as phonetic) Continent*   **Jewelry:** *Pearl Precious*

---

17 泰(214) 平(248) 旅(43) 店(158)

...... Shop
...... Peaceful
...... Travel
...... Peaceful

*Reading from right to left ! ***   **Great Peace:** *Peaceful Peaceful*

---

18 東(203) 華(180) 醫(285) 院(164)

...... Heal. Medical
...... China
...... East
...... Hall

*Reading from right to left ! ***   **China:** *(Far) East China*

---

19 金(96) 山(86) 時(181) 報(134)

...... Mountain
...... Time
...... Newspaper
...... Gold

San Francisco: *Gold Mountain*   **Newspaper:** *Time Newspaper*

---

20 恭(287) 喜(256) 發(288) 財(269)

Wishing Joy: *Respectful Joy*   **Happy New Year!** *Gung Hay Fat Choy !
(Wishing Joy and Expanding Wealth!}*

---

* See explanation at Footnote on page W 3.

Practice Page

Write the correct character numbers on the dotted lines.

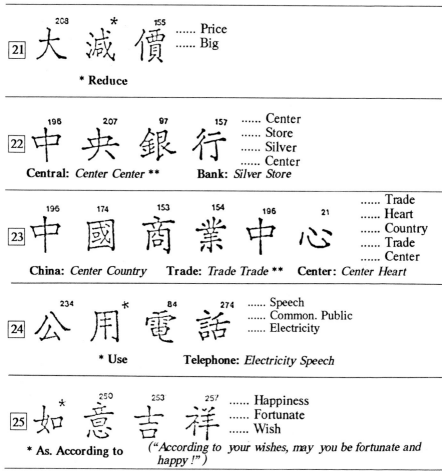

21. 大 減 價
    208 * 155
    ...... Price
    ...... Big

    * Reduce

22. 中 央 銀 行
    196 207 97 157
    ...... Center
    ...... Store
    ...... Silver
    ...... Center

    Central: *Center Center ** *   **Bank:** *Silver Store*

23. 中 國 商 業 中 心
    196 174 153 154 196 21
    ...... Trade
    ...... Heart
    ...... Country
    ...... Trade
    ...... Center

    China: *Center Country*   **Trade:** *Trade Trade ** *   **Center:** *Center Heart*

24. 公 用 電 話
    234 * 84 274
    ...... Speech
    ...... Common. Public
    ...... Electricity

    * Use   **Telephone:** *Electricity Speech*

25. 如 意 吉 祥
    * 250 253 257
    ...... Happiness
    ...... Fortunate
    ...... Wish

    * As. According to   *("According to your wishes, may you be fortunate and happy !")*

26. 米 酒
    106 115
    ...... Wine
    ...... Rice

** Chinese characters are monosyllabic – they are pronounced with one syllable only. For clarity of speech, many "words" consist of two or more characters, sometimes synonyms (characters with the same meanings).

大減價 sale 大減價 sale 大減價 sale 大減價 sale 大減價

21

CENTRAL BANK

中 央 銀 行

22

中國商業中心

CHINA TRADE CENTER

SAN FRANCISCO CHINATOWN

23

公用電話 公用電話

24

如 吉 祥 意

25

MICHIU

米酒

26

Practice Page

Write the correct character numbers on the dotted lines.

27

180	166	115	162
華	園	酒	家

...... Wine
...... House(hold)
...... China
...... Garden

28

179 *	**	105	158
京	滬	飯	店

* Capital = Beijing. ** Shanghai

...... Meal
...... Shop
...... Capital

29

68	166	105	158
花	園	飯	店

...... Garden
...... Shop
...... Meal
...... Flower

30

248	166
平	園

...... Garden
...... Peaceful

Let us assume that the photos on the next pages are photos that you
took yourself during a walk through Chinatown. After you received
them from the printer, you want to know the meanings of the characters. Now you have to use the Character Finder (the *shaded pages
A to F, just before the Dictionary*).

In order to use the Character Finder, you have to know the number
of strokes that each character contains. Please, turn now to: *How to
Use the Character Finder and to Find a Character in this Book* on
pages P34 to P35. To make it easy for you, the characters in the photos
are printed below in the form that you are familiar with. Having found
their meanings, you should enter them on the dotted lines below.

32 東風書店 A B C D	A... B... C... D...
33 女男 A B	A... B...
34 愛心 A B	A... B...
35 北平園 A B C	A... B... C...
36 塲車 A B	A... B...
37 字典 A Records	A...
38 寶謙昌 A Modest C	A... C...

<u>NOTE</u>: Photo No. 31 can be found on page P32.

33

WOMEN 女 ←

男 MENS RESTROOM →

32

東園書店
EASTWIND BOOKS & ARTS

愛心
HEALTHCARE
PROVIDERS.INC.

34

北平園

36

車塲

Parking Rates
1/2 Hour $2.25
Ea. Add. 1/2 hr. .. $2.25
Max. 24 Hours ..$13.00

PU

35

37

The Five Thousand
Dictionary
Chinese-English
C. H. Fenn

字典

A Harvard Paperback
$7.95

38

SUPERIOR
TRADING
CO.

寶謙昌

藥材 参茸

It would not be a bad idea to circle or highlight in the Character Finder all the characters that you already know. This will make it 'custom-made' for you.

Many times, you can judge the number of strokes of a character by just looking at it, or by using your finger to write in the air. For example, you know by looking at it that No. 40A consists of three strokes, and that No.39C has four strokes. Also, that very complex characters like No. 42A and No.43B belong to the last portion of the Complex Group (Table F).

This means that it is not always necessary for you to count the number of strokes.

| 39 | 永 A | 新 B | 公 C | 司 D | A....................
B....................
C....................
D.................... |
| | 瓜 Melon | 菜 E | 雜 Assorted | 貨 F | E....................
F.................... |

| 40 | 上 A | 海 B | | | A....................
B.................... |

| 41 | 金 A | 門 B | 素 Simple | 食 C | A....................
B....................
C....................
Vegetarian: *Simple Food* |

| 42 | 藥 A | 房 House | | | A.................... |

| 43 | 萬 A | 壽 B | 無 C | 疆 Boundary | *Reading from right to left:*
A....................
B....................
C.................... |

| 44 | 華 A | 廚 B | | | A....................
B.................... |

THE CHINESE FORTUNE CALENDAR

© K. DARE 1987

1128 CLAY STREET, SAN FRANCISCO, CA 94108
TEL: (415) 474-1768

Practice Page

Write the correct meanings on the dotted lines.*

⁶¹ 龍	⁴⁷ 犬 ....
⁵⁷ 蛇	⁵⁸ 猪 ....
⁵⁴ 馬	⁶⁰ 鼠 ....
⁵⁰ 羊	⁴⁸ 牛 ....
⁵⁹ 猴	⁵² 虎 ....
⁶² 鶏	⁵³ 兔 ....

* *For the correct answers, see "The Chinese Fortune Calendar" on the previous page. You may also want to write down their ancestral forms.*

How to Use the Character Finder and to Find a Character in this Book.

In the Character Finder *(shaded pages A to F before the Dictionary)*, the characters in this book are arranged according to the number of their "strokes". A "stroke" is a "straight line" produced by the writing brush without lifting it from the paper.

There are exceptions, however, where a stroke is not a straight line. A stroke can be a "hook", when the brush after writing from left to right, continues writing downward, as in B and C in the example below and as in the first stroke of **Woman** in the example on the next page.

The character 永 for **Perpetually (Always, Forever)**, is a good example of how to write a character and arrive at the number of strokes it consists:

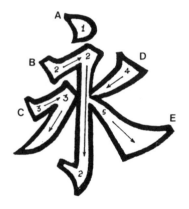

It looks as if this character consists of many strokes, but it actually has only *five* strokes.

This is because B is one stroke only, and so is C. In both cases namely, the writing brush manages to make the "hook" in one continuous movement, without lifting it from the paper.

Can you find the number of strokes of the following characters ?

女	日	金	園	福	愛
Woman	Sun	Gold	Garden	Good luck	Love

You find the answers on the next page !

The number of strokes in a character can best be found by actually writing the character, even if we do so using our finger writing in the air.

There are only a few simple rules to follow. As a rule, strokes are written from from top to bottom or from left to right *. And a character is either built up from left to right or from top to bottom.

The following diagrams should illustrate above rules:

Numbers are the numbers of strokes written so far.
Asterisks (*) are placed near "hooks".

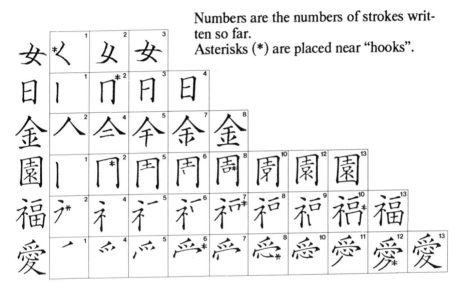

If you can not find the character in the Character Finder, check it in the group with one stroke more or in the group with one stroke less.

In some cases, a character can easily be found without going into the trouble of counting the number of strokes, by looking it up in the appropriate section: **Simple, Intermediate** or **Complex.**

* Unless you are writing with a writing brush, the direction of writing is not of importance. Writing with a brush, it is very important whether you write a stroke from left to right or from right to left, because the resulting "picture" could be very different. For example, to get a stroke that looks the same as D in the example on the previous page, you have to write it from *right to left.*

CHARACTER FINDER

CHARACTERS ARRANGED BY STROKE COUNT

A

Simple

1 一 [1]	**2** 二 [2]	八 [8]	刀 [116]
One	Two	Eight	Knife

力 [19]	十 [10]	九 [9]	七 [7]	人 [32]	入 [237] **3**	三 [3]
Strength	Ten	Nine	Seven	Man	Enter	Three

小 [209]	川 [87]	口 [20]	山 [86]	上 [197]	下 [198]	工 [138]
Small	River	Mouth	Mountain	Above	Below	Work

千 [12]	子 [35]	士 [38]	土 [85]	大 [208]	久 [184]	夕 [189]
Thousand	Child	Scholar	Earth	Big.Great	Long.Lasting	Evening

女 [34]	丸 [118]	**4** 心 [21]	火 [78]	水 [77]	化 [279]	六 [6]
Woman	Pill	Heart	Fire	Water	Change	Six

元 [148]	父 [36]	分 [186]	公 [234]	今 [182]	犬 [47]	日 [73]
Primary.Dollar	Father	Divide.Minute	Public.Common	Now	Dog	Sun

月 [74]	王 [44]	五 [5]	天 [76]	不 [277]	方 [233]	文 [270]
Moon	King	Five	Heaven	Not.No	Square	Writing.Literature

内 [199]	少 [15]	止 [240]	支 [64]	木 [63]	友 [39]
Inside.Within	Few	Stop	Branch	Tree.Wood	Friend

B

井[117]	中[196]	午[188]	牛[48]	手[22]	毛[23]	**5** 加[140]
Well	Center	Noon	Ox	Hand	Hair	Add

北[200]	外[206]	永[185]	冬[195]	司[139]	石[123]	右[205]
North	Outside	Forever.Always	Winter	Manage	Stone	Right

左[204]	布[122]	包[121]	平[248]	半[14]	母[37]	市[178]
Left	Cloth	Wrap	Peaceful	Half	Mother	Market

立[241]	玉[124]	正[226]	古[222]	去[238]	世[246]	出[239]
Stand	Jade	Correct	Age-old	Go.Leave	World	Go out

本[65]	禾[66]	田[119]	目[27]	甘[220]	四[4]	民[40]
Root.Origin	Grain	Field	Eye	Sweet	Four	The people

央[207]	皮[28]	矢[120]	白[98]	生[280]		
Center	Skin	Arrow	White	Grow.Live		

Intermediate

竹[67] Bamboo	多[16] Many	

行[157] Store	好[215] Good	合[149] Agree	全[216] Complete	吉[253] Lucky	字[271] Character	安[252] Peaceful
至[183] Until	早[187] Morning	共[18] Share	后[46] Empress	光[79] Light	虫[49] Worm.Insect	耳[25] Ear
百[11] Hundred	西[202] West	肉[110] Meat.Flesh	年[191] Year	米[106] Rice	血[26] Blood	羊[50] Sheep
舌[24] Tongue	利[156] Profit	豆[109] Bean	言[273] Word	豕[51] Boar.Pig	每[17] Every.Each	花[68] Flower
男[33] Male. Man	貝[125] Shell	局[171] Office	君[45] Ruler	足[29] Foot	車[126] Carriage	
河[88] River	明[217] Bright	門[127] Door.Gate	服[131] Clothes	和[249] Harmonious	物[128] Thing.Object	京[179] Capital
金[96] Gold	空[235] Empty.Sky	昌[254] Prosperous	易[143] Exchange	青[99] Green	直[227] Straight(forward)	店[158] Shop

Section markers: [6], [7], [8]

D

雨 [83]	虎 [52]	夜 [190]	東 [203]	兔 [53]	信 [9] [276]	保 [150]
Rain	Tiger	Night	East	Hare.Rabbit	Faith	Protect
洲 [94]	洋 [93]	秋 [194]	紅 [100]	計 [141]	食 [103]	品 [129]
Continent	Ocean	Autumn	Red	Calculate	Food	Product.Goods
茶 [114]	室 [160]	星 [75]	春 [192]	泉 [89]	界 [247]	香 [221]
Tea	Room	Star	Spring	Spring.Fountain	Boundary	Fragrant
美 [218]	風 [81]	屋 [161]	南 [201]	面 [30]	飛 [243]	
Beautiful	Wind	House.Room	South	Face	Fly	
健 [10] [232]	海 [92]	酒 [115]	院 [164]	祥 [257]	旅 [43]	時 [181]
Strong.Healthy	Sea	Wine.Liquor	Courtyard.Hall	Good luck	Traveler	Time
珠 [136]	都 [173]	強 [231]	航 [244]	料 [142]	粉 [111]	財 [269]
Pearl	Metropolis	Strong	Navigate	Raw material	Flour	Wealth
記 [275]	針 [133]	高 [210]	華 [180]	宮 [168]	家 [162]	泰 [214]
Remember.Notes	Needle	High	China	Palace	Household	Extreme.Peaceful
亞 [236]	夏 [193]	恭 [287]	書 [132]	通 [242]	馬 [54]	島 [95]
Inferior	Summer	Respectful	Book	Go through	Horse	Island

Complex

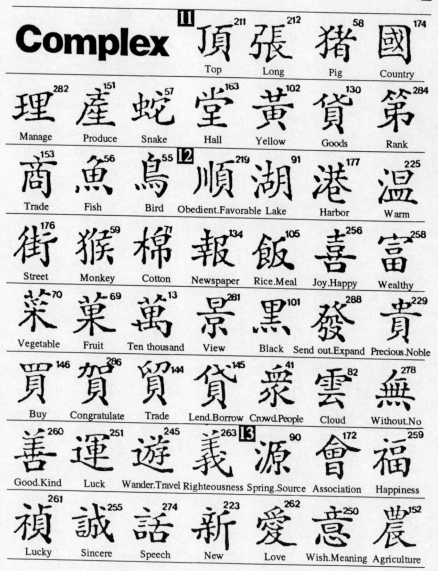

11	頂 (211) Top	張 (212) Long	猪 (58) Pig	國 (174) Country
理 (282) Manage	產 (151) Produce	蛇 (57) Snake	堂 (163) Hall	黃 (102) Yellow	貨 (130) Goods	第 (284) Rank
商 (153) Trade	魚 (56) Fish	鳥 (55) Bird	**12** 順 (219) Obedient.Favorable	湖 (91) Lake	港 (177) Harbor	溫 (225) Warm
街 (176) Street	猴 (59) Monkey	棉 (71) Cotton	報 (134) Newspaper	飯 (105) Rice.Meal	喜 (256) Joy.Happy	富 (258) Wealthy
菜 (70) Vegetable	菓 (69) Fruit	萬 (13) Ten thousand	景 (281) View	黑 (101) Black	發 (288) Send out.Expand	貴 (229) Precious.Noble
買 (146) Buy	賀 (286) Congratulate	貿 (144) Trade	貸 (145) Lend.Borrow	眾 (41) Crowd.People	雲 (82) Cloud	無 (278) Without.No
善 (260) Good.Kind	運 (251) Luck	遊 (245) Wander.Travel	義 (263) **13** Righteousness	源 (90) Spring.Source	會 (172) Association	福 (259) Happiness
禎 (261) Lucky	誠 (255) Sincere	話 (274) Speech	新 (223) New	愛 (262) Love	意 (250) Wish.Meaning	農 (152) Agriculture

F

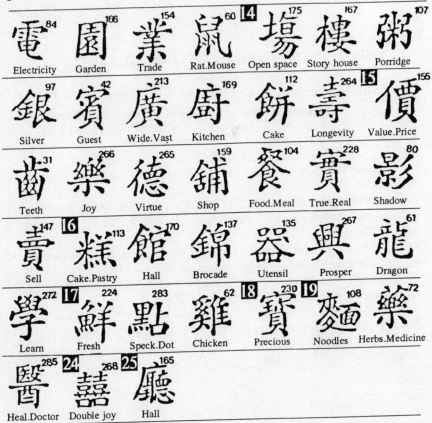

電 84 Electricity	園 166 Garden	業 154 Trade	鼠 60 Rat.Mouse	14 塲 175 Open space	樓 167 Story house	粥 107 Porridge
銀 97 Silver	賓 42 Guest	廣 213 Wide.Vast	廚 169 Kitchen	餅 112 Cake	壽 264 Longevity	15 價 155 Value.Price
齒 31 Teeth	樂 266 Joy	德 265 Virtue	舖 159 Shop	餐 104 Food.Meal	實 228 True.Real	影 80 Shadow
賣 147 Sell	16 糕 113 Cake.Pastry	館 170 Hall	錦 137 Brocade	器 135 Utensil	興 267 Prosper	龍 61 Dragon
學 272 Learn	17 鮮 224 Fresh	點 283 Speck.Dot	雞 62 Chicken	18 寶 230 Precious	19 麵 108 Noodles	藥 72 Herbs.Medicine
醫 285 Heal.Doctor	24 囍 268 Double joy	25 廳 165 Hall				

About the pronunciations of the characters

The Mandarin pronunciation (printed in normal type) is followed by the Cantonese pronunciation (printed in bold). For example, the pronunciation of the word "One" (see Character No. 1) is I ("ee" in Mandarin) and **Yat** ("yaht" in Cantonese).

Chinese words are spoken in "tones" and there are four tones, as follows:

Tone No. 1 (no accent in this Dictionary) – an even, flat voice.

Tone No. 2 (indicated by the accent ′) – a rising voice expressing anger: *What !*

Tone No. 3 (indicated by the accent ^) – a successive lowering and rising of the voice expressing a threat or surprise: *Wh-a-t ?*

Tone No. 4 (indicated by the accent `) – a brief, resolute lowering of the voice as in a strong affirmation: *Yes !*

NOTE: The correct accents for Tone No. 1 and Tone No.3 should be: ‾ and ˇ , but these accents are missing on my computer.

Dictionary of
288 Common Characters
explained by their ancestral forms

NUMBERS

One. One stroke. I. **Yàt** W13. Photo 6		一	一	1
Two. Two strokes. Érh. **Yih** W13		二	二	2
Three. Three strokes. San. **Saàm** W13		三	三	3
Four. A quantity that can be divided into two equal portions. Szù. **Sei** W13. Photos E. 12		四	四	4
Five. Symbol for a unit. (Five is a unit in China, e.g. as used in the abacus – we have namely five fingers on each hand.) Wû. **Ngh** W13		五	五	5
Six. A quantity that can be divided into two equal portions. (With a dot added to distinguish it from "Four".) Liù. **Luhk** W13		六	六	6
Seven. Symbol for a unit used in divination (with a 'tail' to distinguish it from "Ten" [10]). Ch'i. **Chàt** W13. Photo I		七	七	7
Eight. A quantity consisting of two equal halves. Pa. **Baat** W13		八	八	8
Nine. Almost a unit: a wavy "Ten" [10]. Chîu. **Gáu** W13		九	九	9
Ten. Symbol for a unit. Shíh. **Sahp** W13		十	十	10

1

11	百 百	**Hundred.** A unit —¹ (One) and $\ominus$ [98] (White) serving as the phonetic component (see <u>NOTE 1</u>, below). Paî. **Baak**
12	千	**Thousand.** A unit —¹ (One) and $\grave{\wedge}$ [32] (Man) serving as the phonetic component (see <u>NOTE 1</u>, below). Ch'ien. **Chìn**
13	萬	**Ten thousand.** Picture of a scorpion, with its head $\otimes$, legs and tail 十七? and its 'thousands' of claws $\langle\!\!\!\langle$. Wàn. **Maahn** Photos 7. 43
14	半	**Half.** An Ox $\downarrow$ [46] split into two equal portions 八 , namely by cutting it lengthwise, the way butchers do. Pàn. **Bun**
15	少	**Few.** What is left after taking away $\supseteq$ a little from something that is already small 八 [209] . Shâo. **Shíu**
16	多	**Many.** Many nights (two Moons $\mathcal{D}$ [74]). To. **Dò**
17	每	**Each. Every.** Grass Ψ that occurs everywhere, and Mother β [37] to suggest fertility and abundance. Meî. **Múih**
18	共	**Altogether. To share.** Twenty $\sqcup$ ($++$ [10] connected) hands $\wp\!\!\!\prec$ joined together as in a joined effort. Kùng. **Guhng**

<u>NOTE 1</u>: Many symbols consist of two components: one component gives the general meaning of the symbol; the other is the phonetic component giving an indication of the pronunciation of the symbol.

HUMAN BODY

Muscle. Sinew. Strength. Picture of a muscle in its sheath. Lì. **Lihk**		力	19
Mouth. Picture of the mouth. K'ôu. **Háu**		口	20
Heart. Picture of the heart: the sac opened; the lobes and the aorta are also seen. Hsin. **Sàm** W7. Photos D. L. 2. 23. 34		心	21
Hand. Picture of the hand with the five fingers clearly shown. Shôu. **Sáu**		手	22
Hair. Picture of a bundle of hair. Máo. **Mòuh**		毛	23
Tongue. The tongue ⊬ shown outside the Mouth ⊔[20]. Shé. **Sit**		舌	24
Ear. Picture of the ear. Êrh. **Yíh**		耳	25
Blood. A vase containing blood —. Hsüèh. **Hyut**		血	26
Eye. Picture of the eye. (Originally written horizontally ⊂◻ , it was later written vertically to reduce writing-space.) Mù. **Muhk**		目	27
Skin. The skin being stripped off by a hand holding a knife. P'í. **Pèih**		皮	28

29	足 足	**Foot.** The foot 止 (see No. 240) with the ankle, heel and toes. The symbol ○ represents the pelvis. Tsú. **Jùk**
30	面 圓	**Face.** The face with the nose 自 in the center. Mièn. **Mihn**
31	齒 齒	**Teeth.** The teeth (齒) in an open mouth. The symbol 止 [240] (To stop) is the phonetic component (<u>NOTE 1</u>, on p.2). Ch'îh. **Chí**

PERSONS

32	人 人	**Man(kind). Woman. Person.** The being standing on two legs. (Originally written with the head and arms shown 𣎤 .) Rén. **Yàhn** Photo 2
33	男 男	**Man. Male.** The one that gives his strength (力 [19] Sinew) in the Field 田 [19]. (The female doing her work inside the house.) Nán. **Naàhm** P12. Photo 33
34	女 女	**Woman. Female.** Picture of a woman with a sexy figure. Nû. **Néuih** P12. Photo 33. 15
35	子 子	**Child. Son.** Picture of a baby with the legs still bound in swathes. Tzû. **Jí**
36	父 父	**Father.** A hand 彐 holding a rod / , to express authority. Fù. **Fuh**

4

Mother. Picture of a Woman 𠀉³⁴ with 'breasts' ⌢ added. Mû. **Móuh**			37
Scholar. One with knowledge of all things (between the units One —¹ and Ten +¹⁰). Shìh. **Szî**			38
Friend. Two hands working in the same direction. Yôu **Yáuh**			39
People. Weed that grows in abundance (𠂔 and ⻀ are the small stems and leaves). Mín. **Màhn**			40
Crowd. The people. Multitude. A crowd (𠈌³² Persons) as observed by the Eye ⊂⊃²⁷. Chùng. **Jung**			41
Guest. Person welcomed into the privacy (𠀃 sitting woman hiding her pregnancy with apron) of one's house (⌂ dwelling) and offered a gift (貝¹²⁵, formerly used as money). Pin. **Bàn**			42
Traveler. To travel. Transients (𠈌³² Persons) seeking shelter under overhanging branches ⌂ of a wind-blown tree 屮⁶³ . Lû. **Léuih** Photo 17			43
King. The mediator between Heaven ⎺ , Earth ⎽ , and Man — . Wáng. **Wòhng**			44
Prince. Monarch. A hand 彐 holding a sceptre ╱ , and a Mouth ⊔²⁰ that makes law. Chün. **Kwan**			45
Ruler. Empress. A Person 𠂆³² bending over ╱ giving orders (⊔²⁰ Mouth) to people. Hòu. **Hâu** W14. Photo F			46

5

ANIMALS

47	犬 / 犬	**Dog.** Picture of a dog *(seen from the front)*, showing the two front legs ⼁ and the turned-aside head with the big ear and snout ⼂. Ch'uân. **Hyún** Photo 31
48	牛 / 牛	**Ox. Cow.** Picture of a cow *(seen from behind)*; only the two hind legs and tail + are seen; the head is shown with the horns Ψ. Níu. **Ngàuh** Photo 31
49	虫 / 虫	**Worm. Insect.** Picture of a worm or insect. Ch'úng. **Chùhng**
50	羊 / 羊	**Sheep.** Picture of a sheep *(seen from behind)*, showing the horns Ⅎ , four feet and tail ⼁. Yáng. **Yeùhng** Photo 31
51	豕 / 豕	**Pig. Boar.** Picture of a pig with a long tail. Shîh. **Ch'í**
52	虎 / 虎	**Tiger.** Representing the stripes ⼁ of the animal and Man ⼉³² to indicate that it can stand up like a man. Hû. **Fú** Photo 31
53	兔 / 兔	**Hare. Rabbit.** Picture of a sitting hare. T'ù. **Tou** Photo 31
54	馬 / 馬	**Horse.** Picture of a horse, its mane blowing in the wind. Mâ. **Máh** W9. Photos T. 31
55	鳥 / 鳥	**Bird.** Picture of a bird. Nîao. **Niúh**
56	魚 / 魚	**Fish.** Picture of a fish, showing the head ⼂ , scaly body ⊟, and tail ⼂. Yú. **Yùh**

6

Snake. Symbol for a crawling animal 🔲⁴⁹ (Worm) ; and picture of a snake *(seen from the front)*: only its tail and wide-opened mouth with tongue are seen 🔲 . Shé. **Sèh** Photo 31	🔲	蛇
57

Pig. Symbol for a dog 🔲 (*sitting dog seen from the side)* showing snout, ears and legs; and 🔲 (a particle) as the phonetic component (see <u>NOTE 1</u>, p.2). Chu. **Jyù** Photo 31	🔲	猪
58

Monkey. Symbol for a dog 🔲 (see No. 58) and 🔲 (prince) as the phonetic component (see <u>NOTE 1</u>, p. 2). Hóu. **Hàuh** Photo 31	🔲	猴
59

Rat. Mouse. Picture of a rat, showing head with whiskers 🔲 , legs and tail 🔲 . Shǔ. **Syú** Photo 31	🔲	鼠
60

Dragon. A dragon 🔲 flying towards the sky ⚊ and its wings 🔲 . (It was believed that dragons could fly towards the sky and thereby caused rain.) Lúng. **Lùhng** W9. Photos G. 31	🔲	龍
61

Chicken. Picture of a bird 🔲 and 🔲 (how?) as the phonetic component (see <u>NOTE 1</u>, p. 2). Chi. **Gài** Photo 31	🔲	雞
62

VEGETATION

63 木	米	**Tree. Wood.** Picture of a tree: the trunk | with the branches ⌣ and roots ⌢ . Mù. **Muhk**
64 支	🖐	**Branch.** Originally written 🖐 : it shows a hand 🖐 separating a branch ⊣ from a Tree 米⁶³ . Chi. **Jì**
65 本	米	**Root. Origin.** The lower portion of the Tree 米⁶³, as indicated by the dash — . Pên. **Bún**
66 禾	米	**Grain.** A plant (米⁶³ Tree) with ripening ears hanging down at the top ⌐ . Hò. **Woh**
67 竹	𝍠	**Bamboo.** Picture of a bamboo tree with drooping leaves. Chú. **Jùk**
68 花	𝍠	**Flower.** The portion of plants ΨΨ that has greatly changed ᚦᚴ²⁷⁹ (To change). Hua. **Fà** W14. Photos S. 29
69 菓	米	**Fruit.** A fruit ⊕ in a Tree 米⁶³ ; and the symbol for Grass ΨΨ (see NOTE 2, below). Kuô. **Gwó**
70 菜	米	**Vegetables. Dish (food).** A hand that gathers (⌐ a hand reaching down) grass-like (ΨΨ Grass) plants (米⁶³ Tree) (see NOTE 2, below). Ts'aì. **Choi** Photo 39
71 棉	𝍠	**Cotton.** Material from a Tree 米⁶³ , from which White ⊖⁹⁶ napkin ⋔ (see in No. 122) is made. Míen. **Mìhng** Photo 8
72 藥	𝍠	**Herbs. Medicine.** Herbs (ΨΨ Grass) that restore harmony (米²⁶⁸ Music). Yaò. **Yeuhk** W14. Photos U. 7. 42

NOTE 2: As a rule, symbols dealing with vegetative material have the symbol for Grass ΨΨ added on top.   8

NATURE

Description	Old form	Modern	No.
Sun. Day. Picture of the sun. Rì. **Yaht** W12. Photo R	⊙	日	73
Moon. Picture of a crescent moon. Yüèh. **Yuht** P6		月	74
Star. Sublimated matter ascending ∪ from the Earth 土, to become stars ₒₒ . Hsing. **Sìng** P6. Photo 5		星	75
Heaven. That which expands ⁻ over Mankind 大. T'ien. **Tìn** W3. Photo A		天	76
Water. Liquid. A stream ⌇ with whirls of water 川. Shuî. **Séui** P6		水	77
Fire. A pile of wood burning with flames. Huô. **Fó** P8		火	78
Light. Fire 火, being carried by a Person 人 . Kuang. **Gwòng** P8		光	79
Shadow. Shadows ⋰ caused by bright light (when the Sun ⊖ is High 高 up in the sky). Yîng. **Yíng** P8		影	80
Wind. Motion of air 几 and Insect(s) 虫. (It was believed that insects were born when the wind blew.) Feng. **Fùng** P10. Photo 32		風	81
Cloud. Vapors ⌒ rising to the skies ⁼ and causing Rain 雨. Yün. **Wàhn** P10		雲	82

9

83	雨　雨	**Rain.** Drops of water $==$ falling down from clouds suspended from the sky 禾 · Yǚ. **Yúh** P8
84	電　電	**Lightning. Electricity.** That which extends 乚ﾠ from the Rain and strikes down 乚 · Tièn. **Dihn** P8. Photo 24
85	土　土	**Earth.** The layer 二 from which all things │ come out. T'ù. **Tóu** P2
86	山　山	**Mountain.** Picture of a mountain. Shan. **Saàn** P4. Photos 4. 19
87	川　川	**Stream. River.** A big stream formed by smaller streams. Ch'uan. **Ch'uen** P4. Photo 12
88	河　河	**River.** The symbol for Water 川 77 and 可 (can, may) as the phonetic component (see <u>NOTE 1</u>, p. 2). Hó. **Hòh** P4. Photo 5
89	泉　泉	**Fountain. Spring.** Water spouting up ┬ and expanding evenly 八 · Ch'üán. **Chyùhn** P10
90	源　源	**Source.** Water 川 77 and Fountain 泉 89 that come out from a cliff 厂 · Yüán. **Hyùhn** P10
91	湖　湖	**Lake.** Water 川 77 and 胡 (how? why?) as the phonetic component (see <u>NOTE 1</u>, p. 2). Hú. **Wùh** P6
92	海　海	**Sea.** The symbol for Water 川 77 and 每 17 Every, the bottom part of which is 母 17 Mother, to indicate that the sea is the 'mother' of all waters; and grass 屮 to suggest "abundance". Haî. **Hói** W11, 14. Photos E. T. 40

Ocean. The symbol for Water $\jmath''$ and $¥$ [50] Sheep, as the phonetic component (see <u>NOTE 1,</u> p.2). Yáng. **Yèuhng** P4	洋	洋	93
Islets. Continent. Water $\jmath''$ and three isles ₀₀₀ around which Streams lll[87] flow. The symbol lll could also be interpreted as 'many islets combined', as a large island, i.e. a continent. Chou. **Jàu** W11. Photos O. 16	洲	洲	94
Island. A Mountain $\smile$ [96] in the sea on which Birds 🐦[55] can rest while crossing. Taô. **Dóu** P10	島	島	95
Gold. Metal. Four nuggets $\text{ᵒᶜ}_\text{ᵒᶜ}$ buried ($\wedge$ cover) in the Earth $\pm$ [85]. Chin. **Gàm** W10. Photos G. 1. 4. 19. 41	金	金	96
Silver. Metal 金[96] and ℓ ('defiance': a Person 𐤟[22] who turns around ⲅ in order to look (θ[77] Eye) another person 'defiantly' in the eye), suggesting: silver is malleable ('defies' the action Yín. **Ngàhn** W6. Photos C. 22 of a hammer).	銀	銀	97

COLORS

White. The Sun $\odot$ [13] just rising above the horizon—: the sky becoming "white". Pái. **Baahk**	白	白	98
Green. The color ($\sqcap$ crucible containing substance • colored by heat) of young plants Ψ emerging from the Earth $\pm$[89]. Ch'ing. **Chìng** Photo 15	青	青	99
Red. The color of silk (two 8 cocoons on a spindle ⅄ being twisted into a silk thread) and 工[128] (Work) as the phonetic component (see <u>NOTE 1</u>, p. 2). Húng. **Hùhng** Photo 8	紅	紅	100
Black. Soot ✕ deposited around the aperture ⅅ by a smoky Fire 炎[78]. Hei. **Hàk**	黑	黑	101
Yellow. The fiery glow 灷 (Person 𐤟[22] carrying torch 个) from the Fields ⊕[119] at harvest time. Huáng. **Wòhng**	黃	黃	102

食	倉	**Food.** A pot with contents ⊖, a ladle ⟋ and the symbol ⌒ to suggest 'mixing' (three lines coming together). Shíh. **Sihk** Photos 11. 41
103		
餐	養	**Meal. Food.** Food 倉[103] and to consume 月 (⟋ a hand and 月 a skeleton left after the flesh is consumed). Ts'an. **Chàan** W5. Photos H. T. 8
104		
飯	飰	**Cooked rice. Meal.** Food 倉[103] and a hand ⟋ in motion ⟋ , bringing the food into one's mouth. Fàn. **Faahn** W4. W7. Photos H. L. V. 12. 28. 29
105		
米	米	**Rice.** Four grains of rice, scattered ⟋⟍ due to thrashing ＋. Mî. **Máih** Photo 26
106		
粥	粥	**Porridge.** Rice 米[106] that is thoroughly boiled (弓弓 steam coming from boiling water). Chou. **Juk** W6. Photos H. V
107		
麵	麥圓	**Noodles.** Wheat 麥 (plant 火 with ears ∧∧ ; and 夰 Man 儿[32] with shackles ⌒ who advances, suggesting the grain's relentless development); and ⊙[30] Face as phonetic component (see Mîen. **Mihn** W6. Photos H. V NOTE 1, p. 2)
108		
豆	豆	**Bean.** A simple meal • being served on a stemmed platter 豆 . Tòu. **Dauh**
109		
肉	肉	**Meat. Flesh.** Strips of dried meat, bundled together. Ròu. **Yuhk** Photo 11
110		
粉	粉	**Flour.** Rice 米[106] finely ground (川[186] To divide). Fên. **Fán** Photo 13
111		
餅	倉餅	**Cakes. Pastry.** Food 倉[103] and 并 (two men marching in harmony), pastry being a harmonious mixture of ingredients. Pîng. **Béng** W14. Photo M
112		

Cakes. Pastry. Rice ✻ 106 and ￥ (lamb) as the phonetic component (see NOTE 1, p. 2). Kao. **Gòu** Photo 13	糕	糕	113
Tea. Plants ΨΨ and 余 (I, me) as the phonetic component (see NOTE 1, p. 2). Ch'á. **Chàh**	茶	茶	114
Wine. Liquor. A liquor jar 酉 and its contents ₰ 77 (Water, Liquid). Chîu. **Jáu** W4. Photos B. E. F. G. K. 1. 6. 14. 26. 27	酒	酒	115

OBJECTS

Knife. The ancient form was ⊃ ; later to reduce writing-space the handle was curved upwards. Tao. **Dòu**	刀	刀	116
Well. Pit. A well (the dot •) supplying water to eight sur-rounding fields belonging to eight families. Chîng. **Jéng**	井	井	117
Ball. Pellet. Pill. A Person ⟨ 32 rolling down a cliff ⟩ , suggesting the idea that something has been 'rolled'. Wán. **Yún**	丸	丸	118
Field. Picture of a field with furrows. Tíen. **Tìhn**	田	田	119
Arrow. Picture of an arrow. Shìh. **Ch'í**	矢	矢	120

13

包 121	(glyph)	**Bundle. To wrap.** Picture of a foetus 'wrapped' in the womb. Pao. **Baàu**
布 122	(glyph)	**Cloth.** A napkin ⋔ hanging from the girdle and ⊰[36] (Father) as the phonetic component (see <u>NOTE 1</u>, p. 2). Pù. **Bou**
石 123	(glyph)	**Stone.** A stone O in a cliff ⌐. Shíh. **Sehk**
玉 124	王	**Jade.** Three pieces of jade ☰ on a string ⎮. (*Other explanation:* 玉 the precious gem • that only Kings 王[44] could possess.) Yü. **Yuhk**
貝 125	(glyph)	**Shell.** Picture of a small shell ("cowrie"). Pèi. **Bui**
車 126	車	**Carriage. Vehicle.** A carriage *(seen from above)*: showing the body ⊕, axle ⎮, and wheels ☰. Ch'e. **Chè** Photo 36
門 127	(glyph)	**Door. Gate.** Picture of a 'saloon-door' with the swinging leaves. Mén. **Mùhn** Photo 41
物 128	(glyph)	**Thing. Commodity.** An Ox 牛[48] (a priceless commodity in ancient China) and 勿 (do not) as the phonetic component (see <u>NOTE 1</u>, p. 2). Wù. **Maht**
品 129	(glyph)	**Goods. Articles.** Three objects (口[20] Mouth, used here only as a symbol for an object). Pîn. **Bán** Photo 6
貨 130	(glyph)	**Goods. Commodities.** Things to be exchanged (化[279] To change) for money (貝[125] Shell, formerly used as money). Huò. **Fo** Photo 39

Clothes. Dress. A boat 舟 governed by a hand 又 holding a scepter ⼁ . (There is no satisfactory explanation for the meaning: "clothes, dress".) Fú. **Fuhk**	服	**131**
Book. A hand holding a stylus ⼂ drawing a line | on a tablet △ ; and ⊕ the result of this writing. Shu. **Syù** Photo 32	書	**132**
Needle. The symbol for Metal 金 [96] and a needle ⼂ . Chen. **Jàm**	針	**133**
Newspaper. A criminal (辛 pestle, producing grinding action: 'to offend', 'commit crime against men' 余 [32]) and a hand 又 holding a seal ⼁ : an official announcement (of a judgement). Paò. **Bou** **W** 12. Photos R. 4. 19	報	**134**
Vessel. Utensil. Ware. Four precious vessels (represented by their Mouths ⼝ [20]) guarded by a Dog 犬 [47]. Ch'i. **Hei**	器	**135**
Pearl. A precious stone (玉 [124] Jade) and 朱 (vermillion) as the phonetic component (see <u>NOTE 1</u>, p. 2). Chu. **Jyù** Photo 16	珠	**136**
Brocade. White 白 [98] cloth ⼱ (as in No. 122) with gold and silver embroidery (金 [96] Metal). Chîn. **Gám**	錦	**137**

15

138 工	工	**Work.** The ancient carpenter's square, to symbolize work. Kung. **Gùng**
139 司	司	**To manage. Management. Administration.** A Person Ω [32] bending over 〈 to shout his orders (▽ [20] Mouth). Szu. **Sì** **W**5. Photos I. 5. 10. 11. 39
140 加	加	**To add. Increase.** Strength (⁊ [19] Sinew) being "added" to the Mouth ▽ [20] (namely, while speaking). Chia. **Gà**
141 計	計	**To calculate. To count.** To count (⅋ [273] To speak) to Ten 十 [10]. Chì. **Gai**
142 料	料	**To measure. Material.** Measuring Rice 米 [106] with a peck measure (十 [10] Ten; ⟨ ladle). Liaò. **Líu**
143 易	易	**To change. To exchange.** Picture of the chameleon – the animal that can change its color. Yì. **Yih**
144 貿	貿	**Trade.** Door 門 [127] that is open 𝖄 and money (貝 [125] Shell, formerly used as money) passing through it. Maò. **Mauh**
145 貸	貸	**To lend. To borrow.** Money (貝 [125] Shell, formerly used as money) lent out and a Person 人 [32] recording the loan (⟨ marking pin). Tai. **T'aaì**
146 買	買	**To buy.** To put something of value (貝 [125] Shell, formerly used as money) in a shopping net 网 – after it has been bought. Maî. **Máaih**
147 賣	賣	**To sell.** To take out (出 [239] To go out) something of value (貝 [125] Shell, formerly used as money) from a shopping net 网 – in order to sell it. Mài. **Maaih**

16

Beginning. Dollar. Primary. The upper = portion of a Person 𝄇³². Yüán. **Yùhn**	元	元	148
Agreement. Agreeable. Mouth ⊟²⁰ and harmony △ (three lines joined together in harmony): words spoken in harmony. Hó. **Hahp**	合	合	149
To protect. To guarantee. To protect (𝄇³⁵ Child; and wings of a bird, spread 八 to protect the young) and Person 𝄇³² (the one to be protected). Pâo. **Bóu**	保	保	150
To produce. To produce (生²⁸⁰ To grow) and wrinkles 仌 as found on a baby upon birth. Ch'ân. **Cháan** Photo 10	產	產	151
Agriculture. Hard work (𝄇 two hands; 𝄇 head) at dawn * (⊙⁷³ Sun and 辰 period: 𝄇 woman bending down (cp. 𝄇³² Woman) concealing her menses; 辰 sitting woman with an Núng. **Nùhng** Photo 10 apron).	農	農	152
Trade. Where words (⊟²⁰ Mouth. 言²⁷³ To speak) are spoken Within 冂¹⁹⁹ a room, lasting several days (⊙⊙⁷³ Sun). Shang. **Seùng** W12. Photos N. 9. 23	商	商	153
Profession. Trade. A Tree 木⁶³ crowned with its foliage 丵 symbolizing a person's activity and its outcome. Yèh. **Yihp** Photo 23	業	業	154
Value. Price. The amount determined by the shopkeeper (𝄇³² Person) to cover (襾 stopper on bottle) the merchandise's value (貝¹²⁵ Shell , formerly used as money). Chià. **Ga** Photo 21	價	價	155
Profit. When Grain 禾⁶⁶ is cut (刀¹¹⁶ Knife). Lì. **Leih**	利	利	156

* The symbol for Sun ⊙ coincides with the symbol for head 𝄇 .

157	行	𧗟	**Store. Firm.** Footsteps made by left and right feet: a place where people come and go. Háng. **Hàhng** W6. Photos C. U. 7. 16. 22
158	店	㐁	**Shop. Store.** A dwelling ⌂ in which divination ㊀ is practiced. [Divination is spoken out (㇕[20]) after studying cracks ⊦ developed by singeing tortoise-shells.] Tièn. **Dim** W5. Photos L. S. 12. 13. 17. 28. 29. 32
159	舖	舖	**Shop.** A shed 舍 [four walls ⼝ under a thatched roof 舍 (∧ roof; ⼾ plant)], and 甫 (begin) as the phonetic component (see NOTE 1, p.2). P'ù. **Pou**
160	室	室	**House. Room.** A dwelling ⌂ to which one returns after work (⼋ bird with wings backward, coming down to Earth ⼟[85]). Shìh. **Sàt** P2
161	屋	屋	**House. Room.** A place for a person to relax (⼫[32] Person in sitting position) after work (⼋ bird with wings backward, coming down to Earth ⼟[85]). Wu. **Uk** P2
162	家	家	**Home. Household. Family.** A dwelling ⌂ where Pigs 豕[51] have free entry. (To make sure that they were adequately fed, pigs had the same privileges as dogs today.) Chia. **Gà** W4. Photos B. E. G. K. M. 1. 6. 27
163	堂	堂	**Hall.** Soil (⼟[85] Earth) that is being sheltered in a building 𠆢 (the top portion ∧ represents the crest of the roof; ○ is a window). T'áng **Tòhng**
164	院	院	**Hall. Courtyard. Institution.** A building with many steps ⻖ and 完 (finish) as the phonetic component (see NOTE 1, p. 2). Yüàn. **Yún** Photo 18
165	廳	廳	**Hall. Parlor.** Shelter ⼡ and as phonetic component (see NOTE 1, p.2) 聽 (hear – because musical performance often takes place in a hall). T'ing. **T'eng** W5. Photos H. T. 8
166	園	園	**Garden.** Enclosure ⬜ and as phonetic component (see NOTE 1, p.2) 袁 (long robe – because the long vines in the garden give the impression that the trees put on robes). Yüàn. **Yùhn** W4. Photos B. M. O. 27. 29. 30. 35

Multi-story building. Building ($\overset{63}{\text{木}}$ Tree, Wood) and as phonetic component (see <u>NOTE 1</u>, p.2) (a woman locked up in a lofty palace prison for misbehavior). Lóu. **Laùh** W4. Photos F. 14	樓	樓	**167**
Palace. A dwelling ∩ containing a series of rooms 吕 . Kung. **Gùng** W4. Photos K. 14	宮	宮	**168**
Kitchen. A sheltered place ⌐ where one prepares one's meal ($\overset{109}{\text{豆}}$ Bean; hand; a hand that measures). Ch'ú. **Chèuih** P2. Photo 44	廚	廚	**169**
Restaurant. Hall. A large building (building ∩ with many steps) where Food $\overset{103}{\text{食}}$ is served. Kuân. **Gwún** W12. Photo P	館	館	**170**
Office. Bureau. A place where people work: where words ($\overset{20}{\text{口}}$ Mouth) and hands (span of a hand) are used. Chü. **Guhk**	局	局	**171**
Society. Association. A meeting (three lines coming together) where words (that ∟ which comes out from the Mouth $\overset{20}{\text{口}}$) are spoken at the fireside (smoke outlet). Huì. **Wúi** W12. Photos P. 9. 15	會	會	**172**
Capital. Metropolis. Symbol for city (city ○ and its seal) and (a particle) as the phonetic component (see <u>NOTE 1</u>, p. 2). Tu. **Dòu**	都	都	**173**
Country. Country ☐ with its capital ○ that is defended by weapons (halberd). Kuó. **Gwok** W7. W8. Photos C. U. 23	國	國	**174**
Arena. Open space. Field. Ground ($\overset{85}{\text{土}}$ Earth) and (the sun θ rising ∧ above the horizon ‒ and its rays shining over an open space). Ch'áng. **Chèuhng** W12. Photos N. 36	場	場	**175**
Street. Footsteps and that part of the land $\overset{85}{\text{土}}$ on which people walk. Chieh. **Gàai**	街	街	**176**

177	港	潾	**Harbor.** Water ⅃⁷⁷ in the city (city ○ and its seal 굿) that is used (pair of hands in action 𐠼) by many (⊔ = ⊣⊢⁺¹⁰ = twenty = many) people. Kâng. **Góng** W11. Photo N
178	市	肖	**Market.** An open space ⊓ grown with grass Ψ where one obtains ⟅ one's necessities. Shìh. **Sîh**
179	京	京	**Capital.** Picture of the capital's tower. Ching. **Gìng** P12. Photo 28
180	華	蕐	**Glory. China.** Leaves and flowers on a branch 𐠈 that are expanding 亐 (breath 丂 expanding freely — after passing through an obstacle —) into full bloom. Huá. **Wàh.** W7. Photos B. P. Q. 7. 9. 18. 27. 44

TIME

181	時	暙	**Time.** The Sun θ⁷³ and to measure ⟈ [i.e. 'to measure the pulse' (place on the hand ⟈ indicated by the dash —)] the growth of plants 坐 . Shíh. **Sìh** Photos 4. 19
182	今	今	**Now.** Union △ (three lines coming together) and ㇗ (symbol meaning 'contact'), to suggest that all times unite in the "present". Chin. **Gàm**
183	至	坐	**Until.** A bird with wings backward 𐠰 flying down until reaching the Earth 土⁸⁵. Chìh. **Ji**
184	久	久	**Long(time). Lasting.** A person ⼒³² while walking is hindered by an obstacle ⟍ , thus causing a delay. Chìu. **Gáu**
185	永	沿	**Perpetual. Always.** Representing 'veins of water in the Earth' flowing incessantlly. Yùng. **Wíhng** Photo 39

Outside. Foreign. Divination ⌐ (cracks caused by heating tortoise-shells which then were studied by the fortune-teller) done in the Evening ⩙ [189], not following ("outside") the rules*. Wài. **Ngoih**	外	外	206
Center. A Person ⋔ [32] standing in the middle of space ⊢⊣. Yang. **Yèung** *Photo 22*	朵	央	207

* Interpreting dreams (divination) should take place as soon as possible after awakening, and certainly not be postponed until the evening that day.

ADJECTIVES

Big. Great. A person standing with feet wide apart and with outstretched arms, as if showing how "big" an object is. Tà. **Daaih** *Photos G. 10. 21*	大	大	208
Small. An object split into two small portions. (*Other explanation:* a person standing with feet put together and arms close together, as if showing how "small" an object is: ⼩ – cp. No. 208). Hsiâo. **Síu**	川	小	209
High. Picture of a tower. Kao. **Gòu**	高	高	210
Top. The head 頁 (a nose 自 put on two legs 儿 representing a person's head) of a nail ↑. Tîng. **Díng**	頂	頂	211
Long. Hair ⎰ so long that it is tied with a band – and a brooch ⎞ . Ch'áng. **Cheùhng** *Photo H*	長	長	212

213	廣 廣	**Wide. Vast.** Shelter ⌐ and Yellow 黄 (No. 102): the yellow (the imperial color) room, i.e. the imperial hall, a very large ('wide') hall. Kuâng. **Gwóng**
214	泰 夵	**Peaceful.** A Person 大 [32] struggling (hands) in the Water 水 [77]: a person about to get drowned experiencing peacefulness. T'ài. **T'aai** Photo 17
215	好	**Good. Fine.** When one has a wife (女 [34] Woman) and Children 子 [35]. Haô. **Hóu** P12. Photo 13
216	全 全	**Perfect. Complete. Whole.** A job (工 [138] Work) well done (△ harmony, three lines coming together to form a perfect triangle). Ch'üán. **Chyùhn**
217	明	**Bright. Clear.** When the Moon 月 [74] is shining through the window ⊘ . Míng. **Mìhng** P12. Photo 14
218	美 美	**Beautiful.** As is a big sheep (大 [208] Big; 羊 [50] Sheep) with fully developed horns 丫 . Meî. **Méih** W8. Photo C
219	順	**Compliant. Favorable.** Going with the River 川 [87] flow, and managing to keep one's head 頁 (a nose put on two legs 《) above the water. Shùn. **Seùhn**
220	甘	**Sweet.** The Mouth 口 [20] holding something — sweet. Kan. **Kom**
221	香	**Fragrant.** The Sweet 甘 [220] odor of fermented (∧ vapors) Grain 禾 [66]. Hsiang. **Hèung** W11. Photos N. 6
222	古	**Old. Ancient.** When it has passed from Mouth to Mouth 口 [20] over many (十 [10] Ten) generations. Kû. **Gú**

24

New. To cut (axe*) 'new' branches from the hazel tree ([63] Tree and pestle with grinding action = towards people). New branches of this tree were used to beat criminals.
Hsin. **Sàn** * Representing an axe and a chip of wood . Photo 39 — 223

Fresh. Fish [56] and Sheep [50], which were eaten raw by the ancient Chinese and therefore had to be fresh.
Hsien. **Sìn** W11. Photo T — 224

Warm. Water [77] in a dish and the Sun [73] shining on it.
Wen. **Wàn** — 225

Correct. To stop [240] "rightly" at the appropriate limit — .
Chèng. **Jing** — 226

Straight(forward). Ten + [10] Eyes [27] looking and finding no faullt (— straight angle).
Chíh. **Jihk** — 227

Real. True. Real wealth: having a string of shells (string; [125] Shells, formerly used as money) under one's roof .
Shíh. **Saht** — 228

Precious. Honorable. Costly. A basket containing money ([125] Shell, formerlly used as money).
Kuèi. **Gwai** W10. Photo S — 229

Precious. Precious possessions in one's house : Jade [124] porcelain (earthenware) and money ([125] Shell, formerly used as money).
Paô. **Bóu** W10. Photos T. 16. 38 — 230

Strong. A beetle ([49] Insect) that bounces up in the air (a Chinese refllex bow) and falls on its back .
Ch'iáng. **Kèuhng** — 231

Strong. Healthy. A Man [32] writing (a hand holding a stylus |, writing a line — on a table ∧) regulations for the march (long strides): the commander of the troup.
Chièn. **Gihn** — 232

233	方 方	**Square.** The ancient form was a swastika 卐 , representing a "square" Earth with the four regions. Fang. **Fòng** Photo 10
234	公 公	**Common. Public.** Division ノ乀 and distribution of a private possession (delta cocoon; with the self-enclosed silkworm it gives the idea of privacy). Kung. **Gùng** W3.W5. Photos A. I. 5. 10. 11. 24. 39
235	空 空	**Empty.** A cavern dug out by a laborer (工 138 Work). K'ung. **Hùng**
236	亞 亞	**Inferior. Second.** The symbol 工 138 (Work) badly deformed. (As a rule, this symbol is used as a phonetic component ("Ya"), as in 亞 洲 94 亞 which means "Asia"). Yà. **A** W11. Photos O. 16

TRAVEL

237	入 人	**To enter.** A plant with roots penetrating the soil. Jù. **Yahp**
238	去 去	**To go. To leave.** The lid 大 lifted to show an empty vessel ○ : its content "gone". Ch'ü. **Heui**
239	出 出	**To go out.** New shoots coming out from the mother-plant ⌐. Chu. **Chèut**
240	止 止	**To stop.** Representing the foot at rest showing toe ⌐ heel ∟ and shin ⴖ of a foot. (Cp. the foot in motion in No. 242.) Chíh. **Jí**
241	立 立	**To stand. To set up.** A Person 介 32 standing on the ground. Lì. **Lahp**

Through. Open. To march 辶 [Foot 止 (see in No. 240) and footsteps ⫶] and 甬 (raised path) serving as the phonetic component (see <u>NOTE 1</u>, p.2). T'ung. **Tùng**	通 (seal)	通	**242**
To fly. Picture of a flying crane. Fei. **Fèi**	飛 (seal)	飛	**243**
To navigate. Boat. A boat 舟 and the navigator resolutely standing on both legs 亢 . Háng. **Hòhng**	航 (seal)	航	**244**
To wander. To travel. Proceed 辵 (footsteps ⫶ made by the foot 止 (in No. 29) and 㐬 (person with arms making fluttering motions, swimming aimlesly; and 子 35 (Child)*. Yú. **Yaùh**	遊 (seal)	遊	**245**
Generation. World. Three times Ten ╋ 10, which was apparently man's life's expectancy at that time. Shìh. **Sai** **W**11. Photos D. R. 2	世 (seal)	世	**246**
Boundary. Land (⊕ 119 Field) and separation 八 of Persons 卪 32. Chièh. **Kaaì** **W**11. Photos D. R. 2	界 (seal)	界	**247**

* The symbol 子 35 (Child, with the legs bound in swathes) suggests that the person's legs are not visible because they are under the water.

248	平 / 开	**Even. Peaceful.** The breath ᴐ going through an obstacle — and spreading out evenly 兀 . P'íng. **Pìhng** W11. Photos M. 17. 30. 35
249	和 / 和	**Harmonious.** It is natural ("harmonious") that Grain 禾 66 should be consumed (ㅂ 20 Mouth). Hó. **Wòh** P16. Photo 11
250	意 / 意	**Wish.** Expressing one's intention (心 21 Heart) by one's Words 音 273. Yì. **Yi** P14. Photo 25
251	運 / 運	**To transport. Luck.** The army (assemblage ∩ of Carriages 車 126) proceeding 辶 (⼁ Foot in No. 29; ⼺ footsteps) relentlessly. Yŭn **Wahn**
252	安 / 安	**Peaceful. Safe.** Women ⼥ 34 safe in their houses ⼧ . An. **Òn** P14
253	吉 / 吉	**Fortunate. Lucky.** Achieving good fortune, as foretold (ㅂ 20 Mouth) by a sage (士 38 Scholar). Chí. **Gat** P14. Photo 25
254	昌 / 昌	**Glorious. Prosperous.** Sun ⊖ 73 and Moon ⼣ 74 shining at the same time. Ch'ang. **Ch'eung** P16. Photo 38
255	誠 / 誠	**Sincere. Honest.** To accomplish 成 (a boy † that has reached manhood and can handle the sword ⼽) what one has promised (音 273 Words) . Ch'éng. **Sihng** P16. Photo 3
256	喜 / 喜	**Happy. Joy.** There is music (a hand ⼹ holding a stick — beating a drum on a stand 豆) and singing (ㅂ 20 Mouth). Hsî. **Héi** W8. W10. Photos I. 20
257	祥 / 祥	**Auspicious. Lucky.** Heavenly sign (= heaven; ⼉ emanations from heaven) and peacefulness (羊 50 Sheep). Hsiáng. **Ts'eung** P14. Photos W4. 25

Wealthy. Abundant. Having products ○ of the Field ⊕ [119] stacked up 人 under one's roof ⌂. Fù. **Fu** **W10. Photo S**	富	258
Good fortune. Happiness. Heavenly sign 示 (= heaven; 川 emanations from heaven) foretelling prosperity 畐 (products ○ of the Field ⊕ [119] being under one's roof ∧). Fú. **Fùk** **W9.** Photos W1. W4. W5	福	259
Good. Kind. Benevolent. Dispute (誩 [273] Words) peaceful-ly (羊 [50] Sheep) settled and harmony restored. Shàn. **Sihn** **P16**	善	260
Auspicious. Heavenly sign 示 (= heaven; 川 emanations from heaven) foretelling (⊦ cracks produced by heating tortoise shells studied by fortune-teller) prosperity (貝 [125] Shell, for- Chen. **Ching** merly used as money).	禎	261
Love. To swallow ﻌ (Person 人 [32] breathing in air ≡) af-fectionate feelings down in one's heart 心 [21]. The symbol 夊 means: it is a lingering feeling (夊 [32] Person who slowly ad- Aì. **Oi** W9. Photos W2. 34 vances in spite of an obstacle ⌒).	愛	262
Righteousness. Justice and peace (羊 [50] Sheep) established after a battle (戔 two swords crossing each other). Yì. **Yih**	義	263
Longevity. Praying for long life (口 [20] Mouth; ㇇ hand mak-ing gestures stressing request); white hair (Hair ㇇ [23] that has Changed ㇇ (cp. in No. 279); wrinkles (乏 furrows). Shòu. **Sauh** **W8.** Photos W4. 43	壽	264
Virtue. Kindness. An uprigh heart (直 [227] Staightforward; 心 [21] Heart) when dealing with, 'going out to' (彳 footsteps, in No.157) others. Té. **Dàk**	德	265
Music. Happy. A musical instrument: a frame with a drum *(in the middle)* and bells *(on the sides)*. Yüèh. Lò. **Ngohk. Lohk** **P14. Photo L**	樂	266
To prosper. Two pair of hands ㇇㇇ lifting up an object in a harmonious way (同 agreement: a cover 𠔼 that perfectly fits a vessel's Mouth 口 [20]). Hsing. **Hing** **P16. Photos J. 3**	興	267

GOOD LUCK SIGNS – MISCELLANEOUS

268	囍 囍	**Double Joy.** Joy 喜 [256] repeated twice. Hsî. **Héi** **W8.** Photos W3. W6
269	財 財	**Wealth.** Wealth (貝 [125] Shell, formerly used as money) that was acquired (扌 hand). Tsái. **Chòih** **P14.** Photo 20

MISCELLANEOUS

270	文 文	**Literature. Writing.** Intercrossing lines representing waves of thought. Wén. **Màhn**
271	字 字	**Character.** A Child 子 [35] carefully reared in the house 宀 . *By extension:* a Chinese character, because it generally is the result of careful mixing of smaller units. Tzù. **Jih** Photo 37
272	學 學	**To learn. School.** The Child 子 [35] in darkness (宀 small room) and two hands ⺕ of the master pouring knowledge 爻 to the child. Hsüéh. **Hohk** **W14.** Photo Q
273	言 言	**To speak. Word.** The Tongue 舌 [24] and the sound ═ being produced by it. Yén. **Yìhn**
274	話 話	**Talk. Speak.** Words 言 [273] produced by the Tongue 舌 [24] . Huà. **Wah** **P8.** Photo 24

30

To remember. Record. Horizontal and vertical threads on a loom 己 (giving the idea of "repetition") and Words 言 273. Chì. **Gei**		275
To believe. Letter. The Words 言 273 of a trustworthy person (亻 32 Person). Hsìn. **Seun**		276
Not. No. An upward flying bird with wings backward 不, trying in vain to reach the sky ⌐ . Pù. **Bàt**		277
Not. Without. A multitude (⅏ = ++++ 10 = forty) Men 大 32 clearing a forest (many Trees 林 63)leaving an open space without trees. Wú. **Mòuh** Photo 43		278
To change. A Person 亻 32 and a Person-upside-down 匕 32 : a person who "changed" position. Huà. **Fa**		279
To grow. Give birth to. A plant Ψ growing out from the Earth 土 85. Sheng. **Sàng**		280
View. The Sun ⊙ 73 looking over the Capital 京 179. Chîng. **Gíng**		281
Principle. To manage. A gem (玉 124 Jade) that must be cut according to certain "principles" and 里 (village) serving as the phonetic component (see <u>NOTE 1</u>, p. 2). Lî. **Léih**		282
Speck. Dot. Soot ⋎ deposited by a smoky (黑 101 Black) Fire 炎 78 around a vent ∞, and 卜 (To divine, see in No.158) serving as the phonetic component (see <u>NOTE 1</u>, p. 2). Tìen. **Dím** **W**7. Photo D		283
Rank. Grade. Thread successively wound 弟 on a spool with a winch at the bottom 丿 *(Please, note that the symbol for Bamboo 竹 67 improperly appears in the modern writing.)* Tì. **Daih**		284

31

醫	醫	**Heal. Medical. Doctor.** Taking out (hand making jerky motion) arrow from receptacle, in order to shoot down the demon; and to give elixir (wine jar) to the patient. Yi. **Yi** Photo 18
賀	賀	**Congratulate.** Wealth (貝 125 shell, formerly used as money) to be added 力 口140. Hò. **Hoh**
恭	恭	**Respectful.** Twenty ㅂ (++ 10 ten) pair of hands joined together and held up as when showing respect (心27 heart) to a person according to Chinese custom. Kung. **Gùng** Photo 20
發	發	**Send forth. Expand.** To separate (two feet back-to-back, see in No. 240) the arrow from the bow. Fa. **Faat** Photo 20

285, 286, 287, 288

SUBJECT INDEX

Food 食 103 餐 104
Foot 足 29
Foreign 外 206
Fortunate 吉 253
Fountain 泉 89
Four 四 4
Fragrant 香 221
Fresh 鮮 224
Friend 友 39
Fruit 菓 69

Garden 園 166
Gate 門 127
Generation 世 246
Glorious 昌 254
Glory 華 180
Go 去 238
Go out 出 239
Gold 金 96
Good 好 215 善 260
Good fortune 福 259
Goods 品 129 貨 130
Grade 第 284
Grain 禾 66
Great 大 208
Green 青 99
Grow 生 280
Guarantee 保 150
Guest 賓 42

Hair 毛 23
Half 半 14
Hall 堂163 院164 廳165   館 170
Hand 手 22
Happiness 福 259
Happy 喜 256 樂 266
Harbor 港 177
Hare 兔 53

Harmonious 和 249
Heal 醫 285
Healthy 健 232
Heart 心 21
Heaven 天 76
Herbs 藥 72
High 高 210
Home 家 162
Honest 誠 255
Honorable 貴 229
Horse 馬 54
House 室 160 屋 161
Household 家 162
Hundred 百 11

Increase 加 140
Inferior 亞 236
Insect 虫 49
Inside 內 199
Institution 院 164
Island 島 95
Islets 洲 94

Jade 玉 124
Joy 喜 256

Kind 善260
Kindness 德 265
King 王 44
Kitchen 廚 169
Knife 刀 116

Lake 湖 91
Lasting 久184
Learn 學 272
Leave 去 238
Left 左 204
Lend 貸 145
Letter 信 276

Light 光 79
Lightning 電 84
Liquid 水 77
Liquor 酒 115
Literature 文 270
Long (length) 張 212
Long (time) 久 184
Longevity 壽 264
Love 愛 262
Luck 運 251
Lucky 吉 253 祥 257

Male 男 33
Man 人 32 男 33
Manage 司 139 理 282
Management 司 139
Mankind 人 32
Many 多 16
Market 市 178
Material 料 142
Meal 餐 104 飯 105
Measure 料 142
Meat 肉 110
Medical 醫 285
Medicine 藥 72
Metal 金 96
Metropolis 都 173
Minute 分186
Monarch 君 45
Monkey 猴 59
Moon 月 74
Morning 早 187
Mother 母 37
Mountain 山 86
Mouse 鼠 60
Mouth 20
Nulti-story building 樓 167
Multitude 眾 41
Muscle 力 19
Music 樂 266

Getting the Most from the Flash Cards

On the cards, the most common characters in this book are marked with three asterisk (***). There are 41 characters that appear on the Chinese Menu *(see below)*. To familiarize yourself with them, go to the Character Finder *(shaded pages* **A** to **F**) and find them there*.

Find them also on the Flash Cards (by their Character Numbers). Mark them with a capital M (for *Menu*), before cutting them out. By putting aside the ones that you know, you can concentrate on the ones that you don't know. [Instead of cutting out the cards, you can *circle* or *hi-lite* the ones that you know already].

* Characters with an asterisk (*) are not in this book.

Other characters appearing on the Chinese Menu can be found in my other book *What Character Is That ? An Easy-Access Dictionary of 5,000 Chinese Characters.*

What's On the Menu? – Characters seen on the Menu.

飯	麵	粥	豆	Bean curd (Tofu) 腐	猪	雞	魚
Rice.Meal	Noodles	Porridge	Bean	*Decay**	Pig	Chicken	Fish
牛 Beef	肉	鳥	羊 Lamb	肉	火 Ham	腿	肉
Ox	Meat.Flesh	Bird	Sheep	Meat.Flesh	Fire	*Thigh**	Meat.Flesh
海 Sea Food	鮮	大 Prawn	蝦	龍 Lobster	蝦	包 Steamed bun	菜
Sea	Fresh	Big.Great	*Shrimp**	Dragon	*Shrimp**	Wrap	Vegetable
白 Chin. cabbage (Bokchoy)	菜	竹 Bamboo shoot	筍	生 Lettuce	菜	冬 Winter melon	瓜
White	Vegetable	Bamboo	*Shoot**	Grow.Live	Vegetable	Winter	*Melon**
點 Pastry lunch (Dim Sum)	心	春 Egg roll	捲	雲 Wonton (soup)	吞	油	Pancake 餅
Speck.Dot	Heart	Spring	*Roll**	Cloud	*Swallow**	*Oil**	Cake
五 Five Spice (chicken)	香	宮 Kung Pao (chicken)	保	北 Beijing (duck)	京	湖 Hunan (beef)	南
Five	Fragrant	Palace	Protect	North	Capital	Lake	South
肉 Meatball	丸	木 Mu Su (pork)	須	玉 Corn	米	茶	酒
Meat.Flesh	Ball	Tree.Wood	*Beard**	Jade	Rice	Tea	Wine.Liquor

NOTE: The character for "Pig" 豬 does not appear on the Menu itself; it appears on Menu headings. The character for "Meat" 肉 is used to indicate "Pork", since pork is the staple meat in China.

FLASH CARDS (to be cut out for review purposes)

1 一 *** 6 W13	2 二 *** W13	3 三 *** W13	4 四 *** E. 12 W13	5 五 *** W13
6 六 *** W13	7 七 *** I W13	8 八 *** W13	9 九 *** W13	10 十 *** W13
11 百 ***	12 千 ***	13 萬 *** 7. 43	14 半 ***	15 少 **
16 多 **	17 每 **	18 共 **	19 力 **	20 口 ***
21 心 D. L. 2. 34 W7	22 手 *	23 毛 *	24 舌 *	25 耳 *
26 血 **	27 目 **	28 皮 *	29 足 *	30 面 *
31 齒 **	32 人 *** 2	33 男 *** P12. 33	34 女 P12. 15. 33	35 子 ***
36 父 *	37 母 *	38 士 *	39 友 *	40 民 **

Numbers on Top Right-hand Corners are Character Numbers in the Dictionary.
W 4, etc. refer to Chinatown Chapter. Letters and numbers refer to Photographs.
Commonly seen characters: *** Most common. ** Very common. * Common.

FLASH CARDS (to be cut out for review purposes)

眾 41 **	賓 42 **	旅 43 *** 17	王 44 ***	君 45 ***
右 46 *** F W14	犬 47 *** 31	牛 48 *** 31	虫 49 *	羊 50 *** 31
豕 51 *	虎 52 *** 31	兔 53 *** 31	馬 54 *** T. 31 W9	鳥 55 ***
魚 56 ***	蛇 57 *** 31	猪 58 *** 31	猴 59 *** 31	鼠 60 *** 31
龍 61 *** G. 31 W9	雞 62 *** 31	木 63 ***	支 64 *	本 65 ***
禾 66 ***	竹 67 ***	花 68 *** S. 29 W14	菓 69 ***	菜 70 *** 39
棉 71 ** 8	藥 72 *** U. 7.42 W14	日 73 *** R W12	月 74 *** P6	星 75 *** P6.5
天 76 *** A W3	水 77 *** P6	火 78 *** P8	光 79 *** P8	影 80 *** P8

Numbers on Top Right-hand Corners are Character Numbers in the Dictionary.
W 4, etc. refer to Chinatown Chapter. Letters and numbers refer to Photographs.
Commonly seen characters: *** Most common. ** Very common. * Common.

FLASH CARDS (to be cut out for review purposes)

風 81 ** P10. 32	雲 82 ** P10	雨 83 ** P8	電 84 *** P8. 24	土 85 ** P2
山 86 *** P4. 4.19	川 87 *** P4. 12	河 88 ** P4. 5	泉 89 ** P10	源 90 ** P10
湖 91 *** P6	海 92 E.T.40 W11,14	洋 93 *** P4	洲 94 *** O.16 W11	島 95 ** P10
金 96 G.1.4.41 W10	銀 97 *** C.22 W6	白 98 **	青 99 ** 15	紅 100 ** 8
黑 101 **	黃 102 **	食 103 *** 11.41	餐 104 *** H.T.8 W5	飯 105 *** L.12.28.29 W4,7
米 106 *** 26	粥 107 *** H.V W6	麵 108 *** H.V W6	豆 109 ***	肉 110 *** 11
粉 111 *** 13	餅 112 *** M W14	糕 113 *** 13	茶 114 ***	酒 115 E.K.26.27 W4
刀 116 **	井 117 **	丸 118 **	田 119 **	矢 120 **

Numbers on Top Right-hand Corners are Character Numbers in the Dictionary.
W 4, etc. refer to Chinatown Chapter. Letters and numbers refer to Photographs.
Commonly seen characters: *** Most common. ** Very common. * Common.

FLASH CARDS (to be cut out for review purposes)

121 包 ***	122 布 **	123 石 **	124 玉 ***	125 貝 **
126 車 *** 36	127 門 *** 41	128 物 **	129 品 ** 6	130 貨 ** 39
131 服 **	132 書 *** 32	133 針 **	134 報 *** R.4.19 **W 12**	135 器 **
136 珠 *** 16	137 錦 **	138 工 ***	139 司 *** 5.10.11.39 **W 5**	140 加 **
141 計 **	142 料 ***	143 易 ***	144 貿 ***	145 貸 **
146 買 ***	147 賣 ***	148 元 ***	149 合 **	150 保 **
151 產 ** 10	152 農 ** 10	153 商 ***N.9.23**W 12**	154 業 *** 23	155 價 *** 2'1
156 利 **	157 行 *** C.7.16.22 **W 6**	158 店 *** S.12.17.28 **W 5**	159 舖 ***	160 室 *** P2

Numbers on Top Right-hand Corners are Character Numbers in the Dictionary.
W 4, etc. refer to Chinatown Chapter. Letters and numbers refer to Photographs.
Commonly seen characters: *** Most common. ** Very common. * Common.

FLASH CARDS (to be cut out for review purposes)

屋 161 *** P2	家 162 B.E.M.6 W4	堂 163 W4	院 164 *** 18	廳 165 *** H.T.8 W5
園 166 M.O.30.35 W4	樓 167 *** F.14 W4	宮 168 *** K.14 W4	廚 169 *** P2. 44	館 170 *** P W12
局 171 ***	會 172 ***P.9.15 W12	都 173 ***	國 174 C.U.23 W7,8	塲 175 *** N.36 W12
街 176 ***	港 177 *** N W11	市 178 ***	京 179 *** P12. 28	華 180 *** B.P.7.9.44 W7
時 181 *** 4.19	今 182 **	至 183 ***	久 184 **	永 185 *** 39
分 186 ***	早 187 ***	午 188 ***	夕 189 **	夜 190 ***
年 191 *** 15	春 192 ***	夏 193 ***	秋 194 ***	冬 195 ***
中 196 P.U.7.9. W7	上 197 *** P2. 40	下 198 *** A W3	内 199 ***	北 200 *** U.35 W13

Numbers on Top Right-hand Corners are Character Numbers in the Dictionary.
W 4, etc. refer to Chinatown Chapter. Letters and numbers refer to Photographs.
Commonly seen characters: *** Most common. ** Very common. * Common.

FLASH CARDS (to be cut out for review purposes)

201 南 *** U W13	202 西 *** W13	203 東 *** 18.32 W13	204 左 **	205 右 **
206 外 **	207 央 ***	208 大 *** G.10.21 22	209 小 ***	210 高 ***
211 頂 **	212 長 *** H	213 廣 ***	214 泰 17	215 好 *** P12. 13
216 全 ***	217 明 *** P12. 14	218 美 *** C W8	219 順 ***	220 甘 **
221 香 *** N.6 W11	222 古 **	223 新 *** 39	224 鮮 *** T W11	225 溫 **
226 正 ***	227 直 ***	228 實 **	229 貴 *** S W10	230 寶 T.16.38 W10
231 強 **	232 健 **	233 方 ** 10	234 公 *** 5.11.24.39 W5	235 空 **
236 亞 *** O.16 W11	237 入 ***	238 去 **	239 出 ***	240 止 **

Numbers on Top Right-hand Corners are Character Numbers in the Dictionary.
W 4, etc. refer to Chinatown Chapter. Letters and numbers refer to Photographs.
Commonly seen characters: *** Most common. ** Very common. * Common.

FC 7
FLASH CARDS (to be cut out for review purposes)

241 立 **	242 通 ***	243 飛 ***	244 航 ***	245 遊 **
246 世 ***D.R.2 W11	247 界 ***D.R.2 W11	248 平 M.17.30.35 W11	249 和 P16. 11	250 意 ** P14. 25
251 運 **	252 安 *** P14	253 吉 ** P14. 25	254 昌 ** P16. 38	255 誠 ** P16. 3
256 喜 ***I.20 W8,10	257 祥 *** P14. W4.25	258 富 *** S W10	259 福 *** W1.W4.W5 W9	260 善 ** P16
261 禎 **	262 愛 *** W2.34 W9	263 義 **	264 壽 *** W4.43 W8	265 德 **
266 樂 ** P14. L	267 興 ** P16. J.3	268 囍 W3.W6 W8	269 財 *** P14. 20	270 文 **
271 字 *** 37	272 學 *** Q W14	273 言 *	274 話 *** P8. 24	275 記 **
276 信 **	277 不 ***	278 無 ** 43	279 化 **	280 生 ***

Numbers on Top Right-hand Corners are Character Numbers in the Dictionary.
W 4, etc. refer to Chinatown Chapter. Letters and numbers refer to Photographs.
Commonly seen characters: *** Most common. ** Very common. * Common.

FLASH CARDS (to be cut out for review purposes)

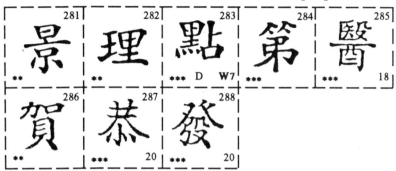

Numbers on Top Right-hand Corners are Character Numbers in the Dictionary.
W 4, etc. refer to Chinatown Chapter. Letters and numbers refer to Photographs.
Commonly seen characters: *** Most common. ** Very common. * Common.